Imprint

Holger Nils Pohl
Dellbrücker Hauptstraße 74
51069 Köln
Germany

ISBN 978-3-9821200-3-4

THE SECOND 100 DAILY DRAWINGS

The first book *100 Daily Drawings* developed from a solidarity event I and my team hosted during 2020 to keep people creative throughout a time of digital transformation. But soon after I published the book, the first voices became public. You couldn‘t get enough. So Beni and I sat down and created *100 Daily Drawings Vol.2*. It could have been *100 more Daily Drawings* or *101-200 Daily Drawings* or what not. We made it plain simple. Not all drawings in this book are plain simple, though. As with the first book, we have varied the difficulty of the drawings. That is not to put you off, but to get you out of your comfort zone while recognizing that you can actually draw!

I believe that drawing can solve lots of your challenges. Don't postpone it any further by reading these lines. Go ahead, grab a pen and get that first drawing on paper!

Yours,

DAY 1

Hello again!

DAY 2

Jumping

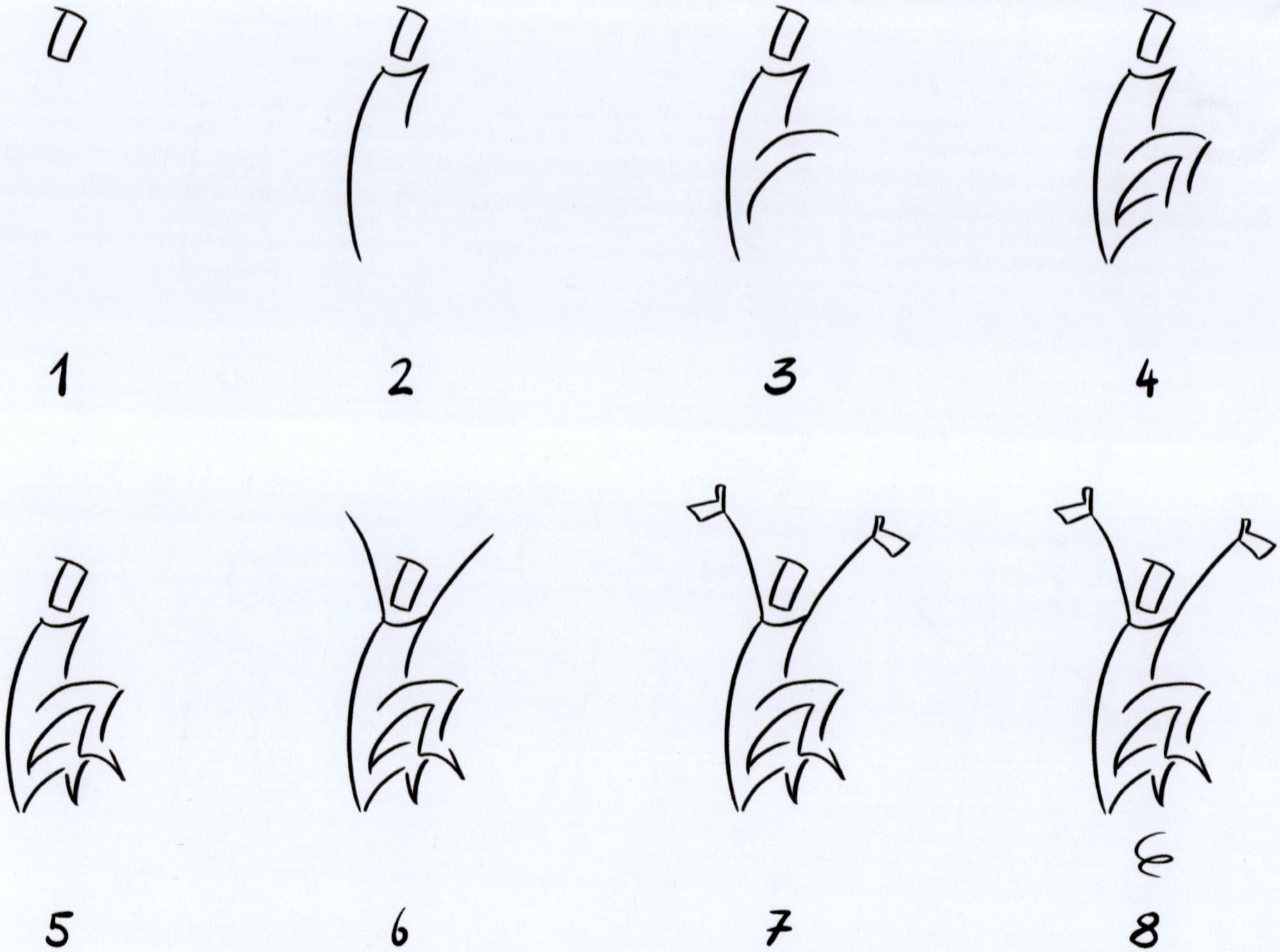

DAY 3

Cow

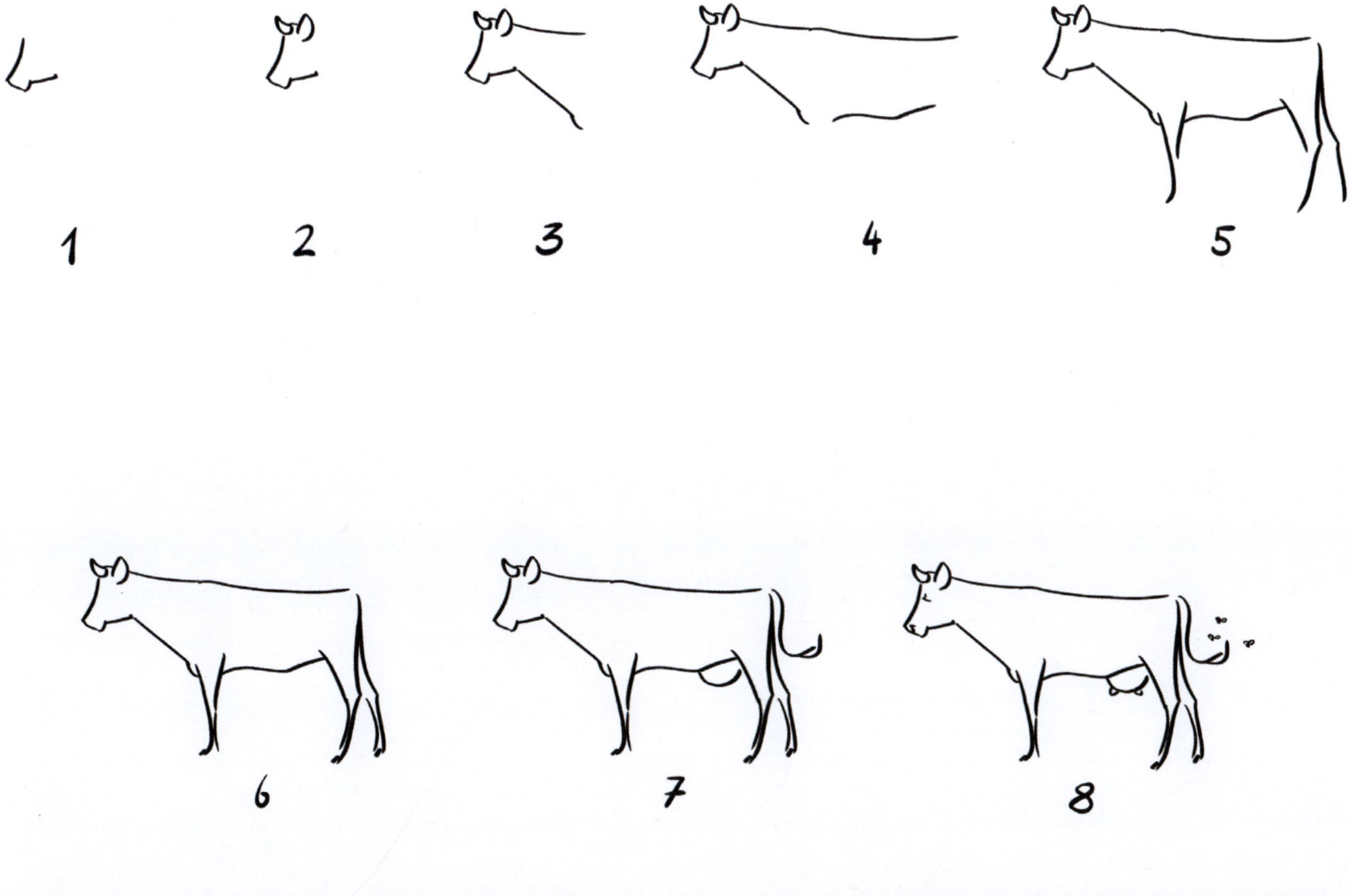

DAY 4

Bowl of soup

DAY 5

Golf

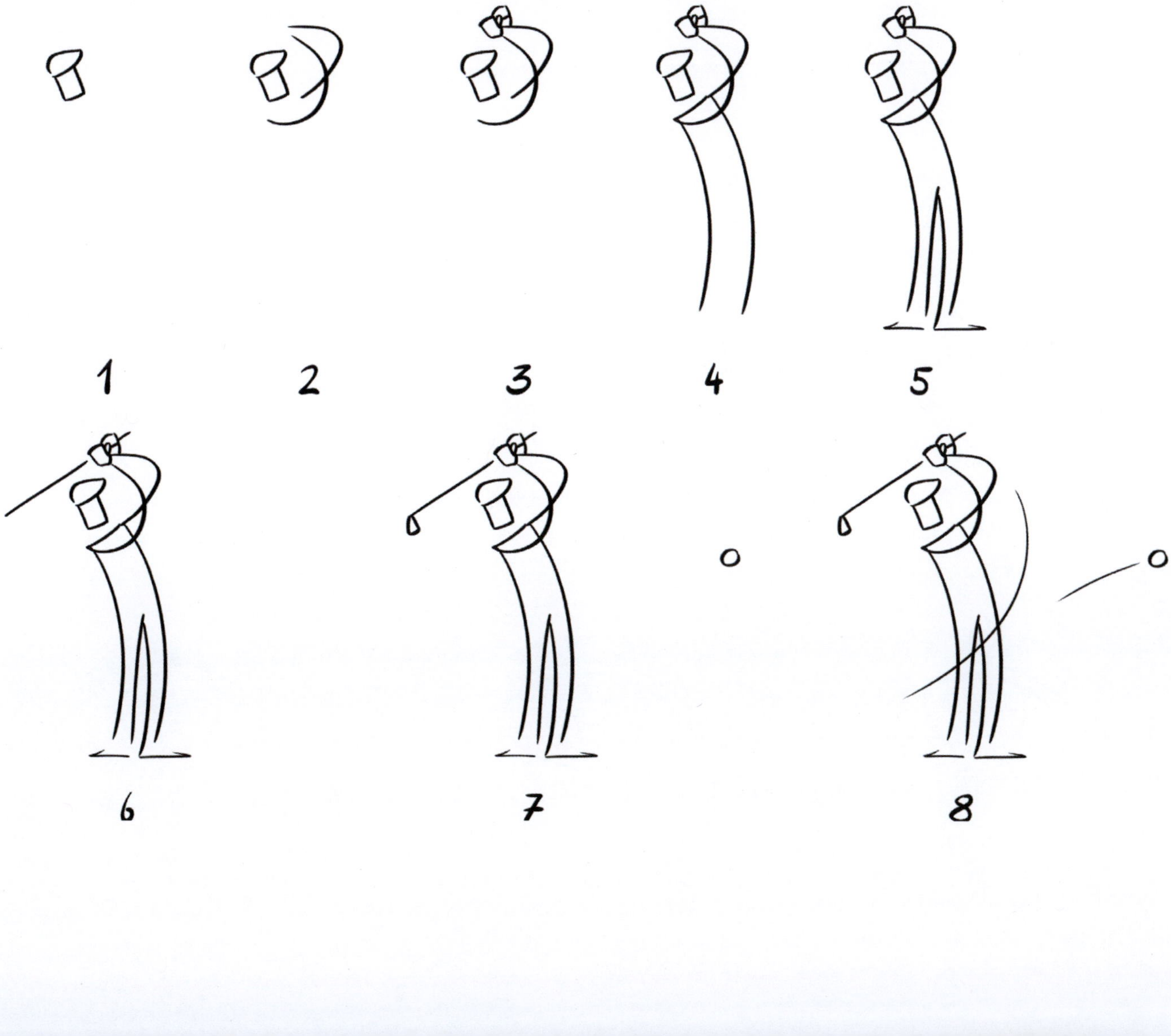

DAY 6

Eye

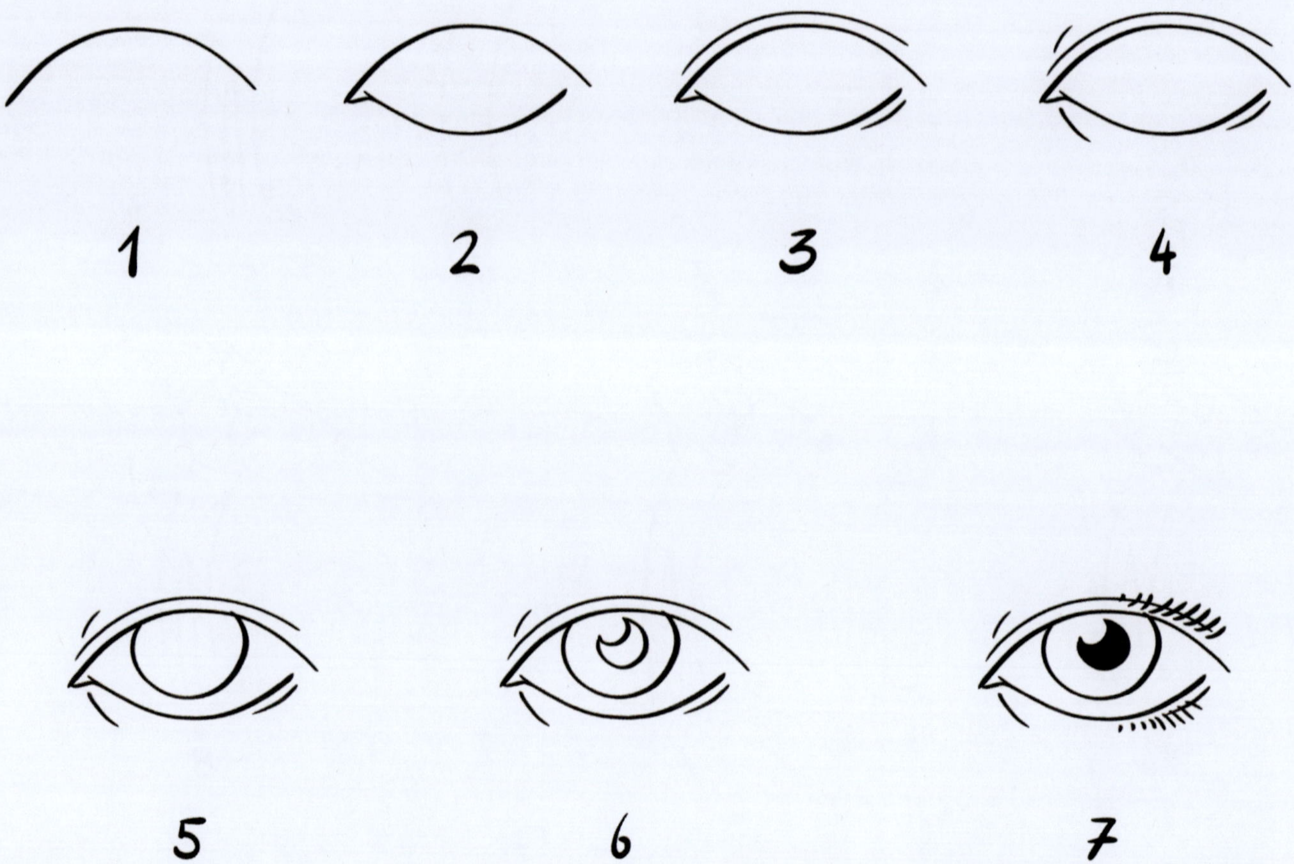

DAY 7

Cactus

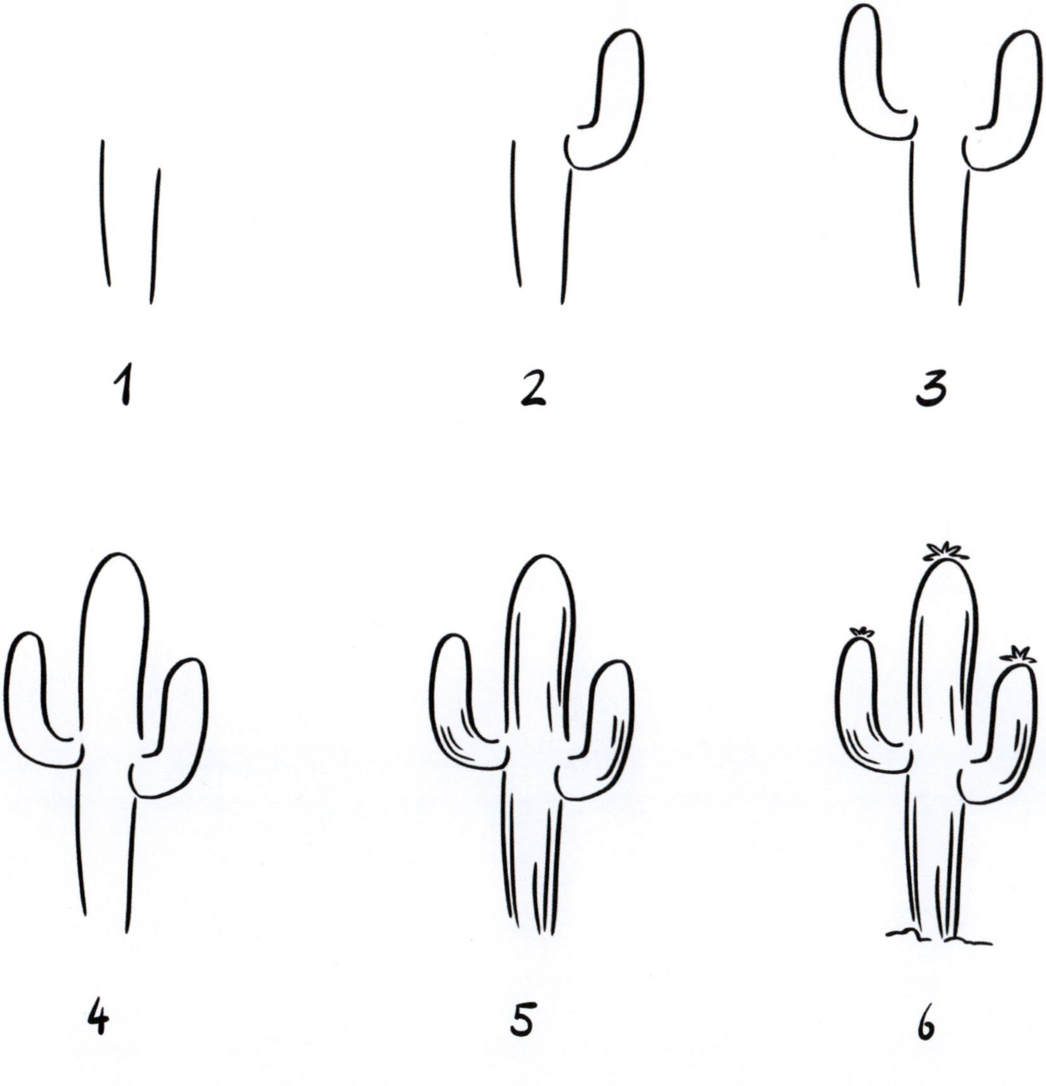

DAY 8

Flamingo

1

2

3

4

5

6

7

DAY 9

Cocktail

DAY 10

Lantern

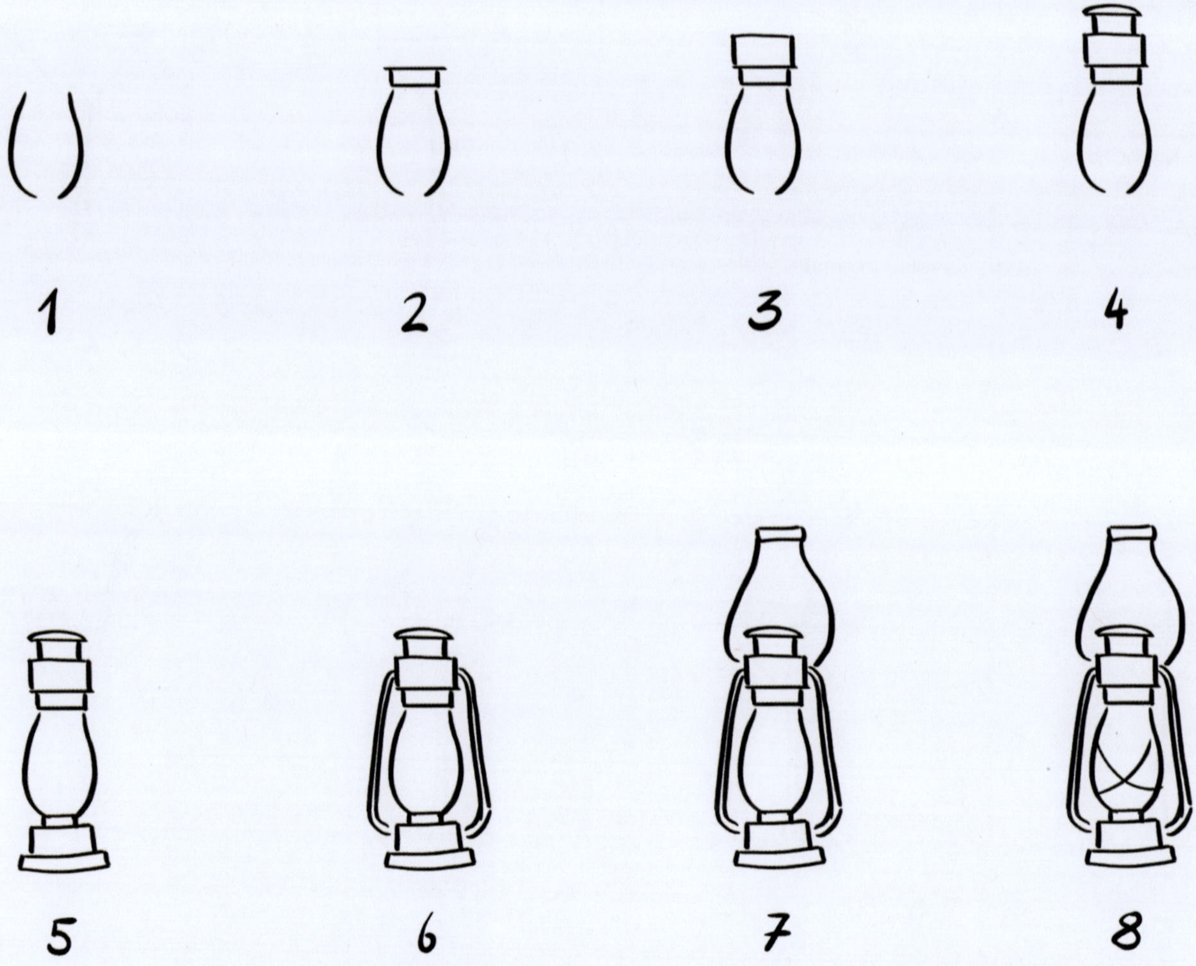

DAY 11

Anchor

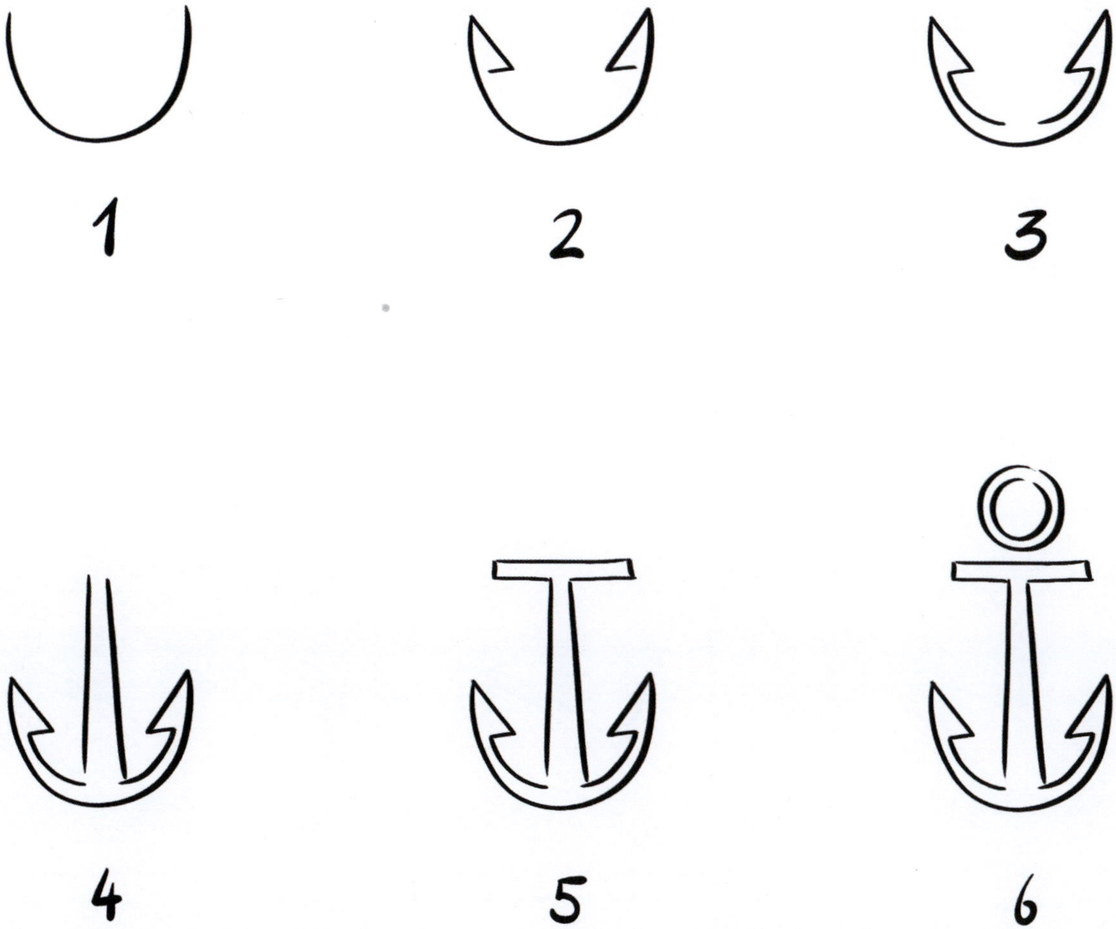

DAY 12

Bell

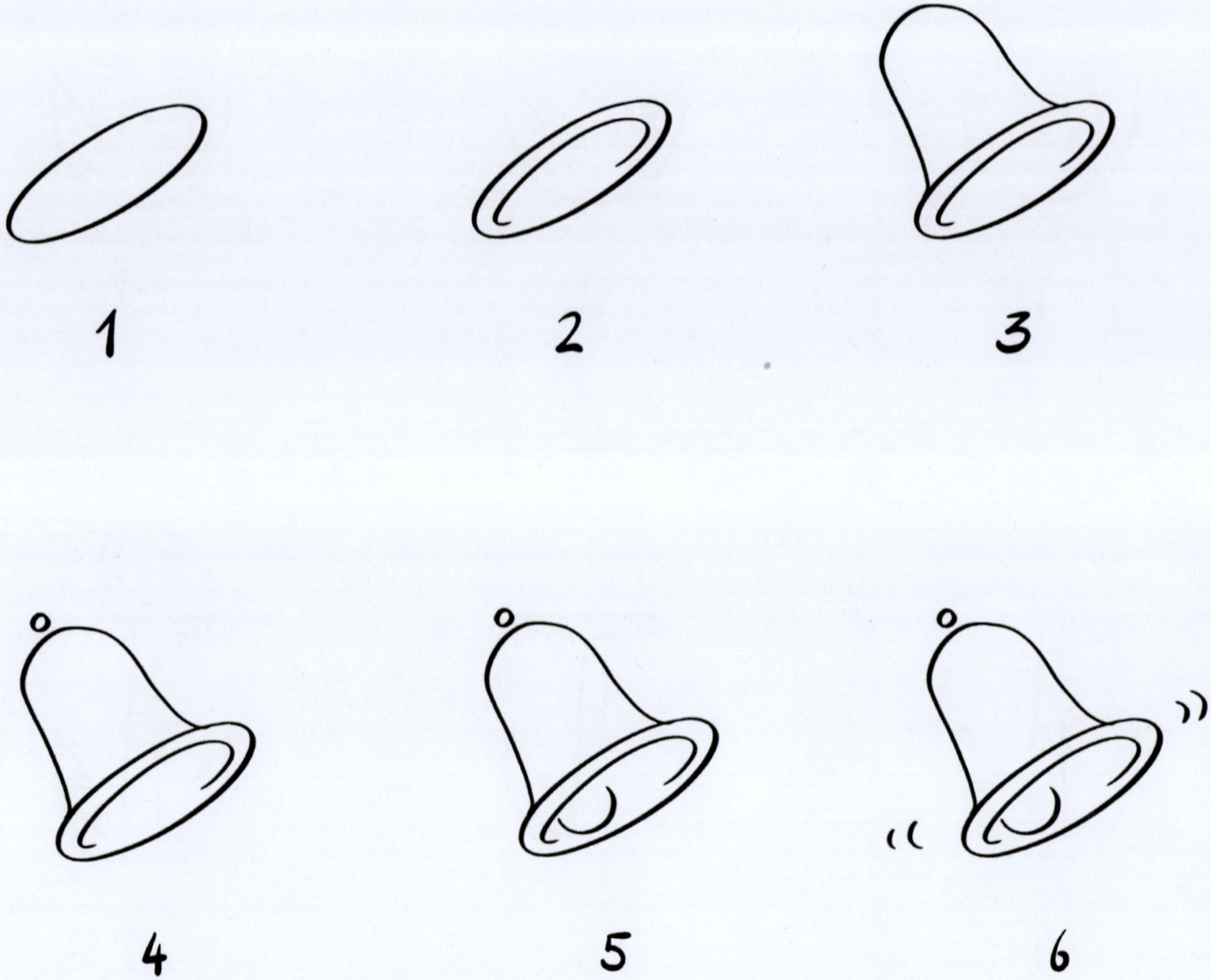

DAY 13

Tree

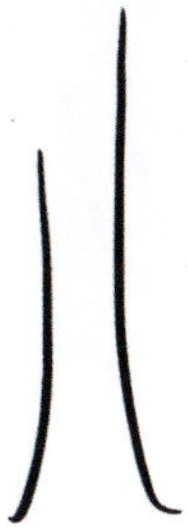

1

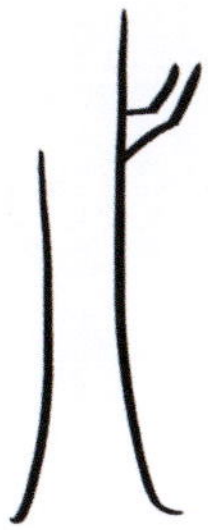

2

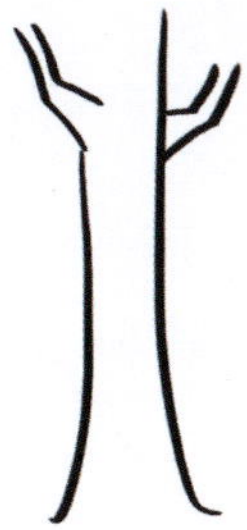

3

4

5

6

DAY 14

Ear

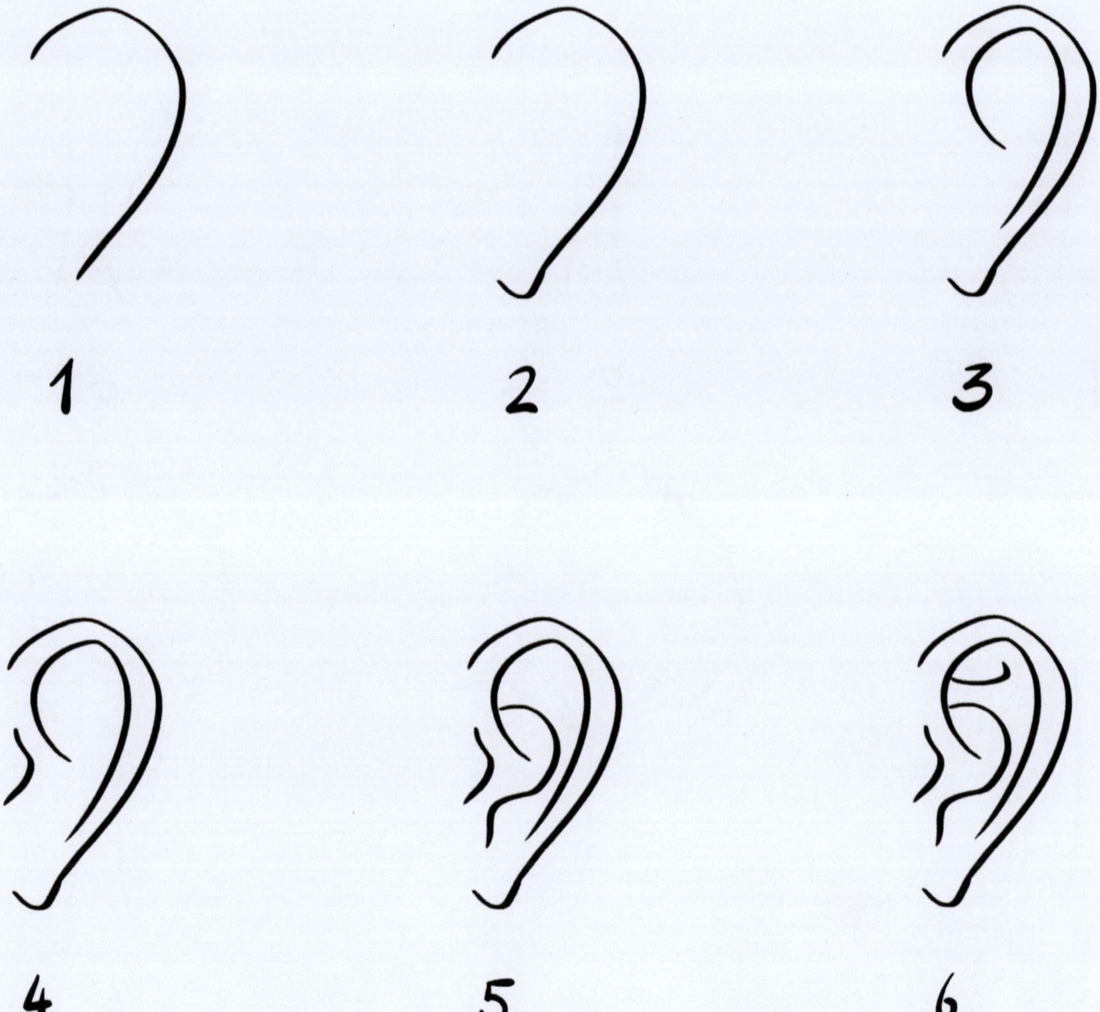

DAY 15

Digging

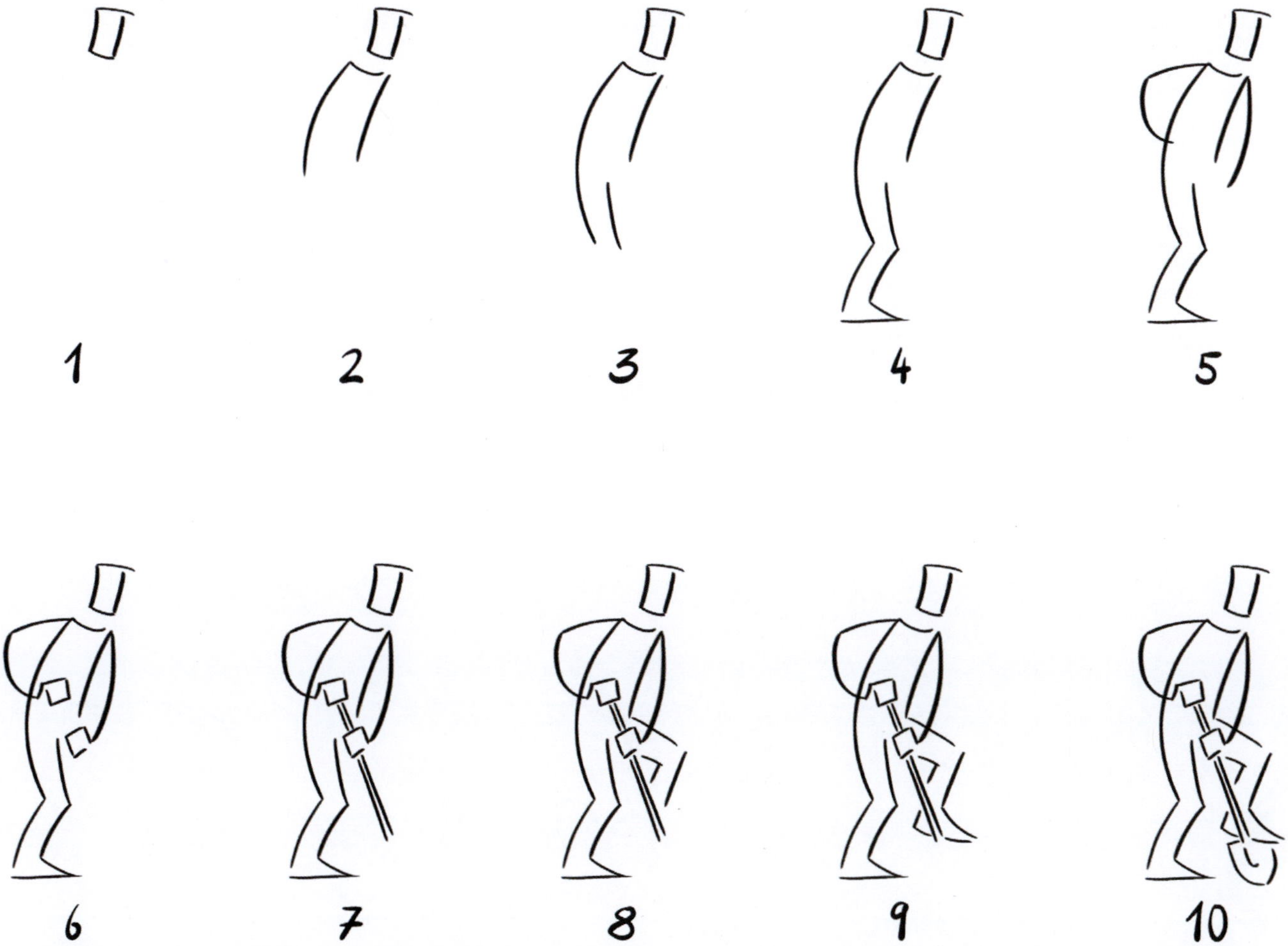

DAY 16

Pig

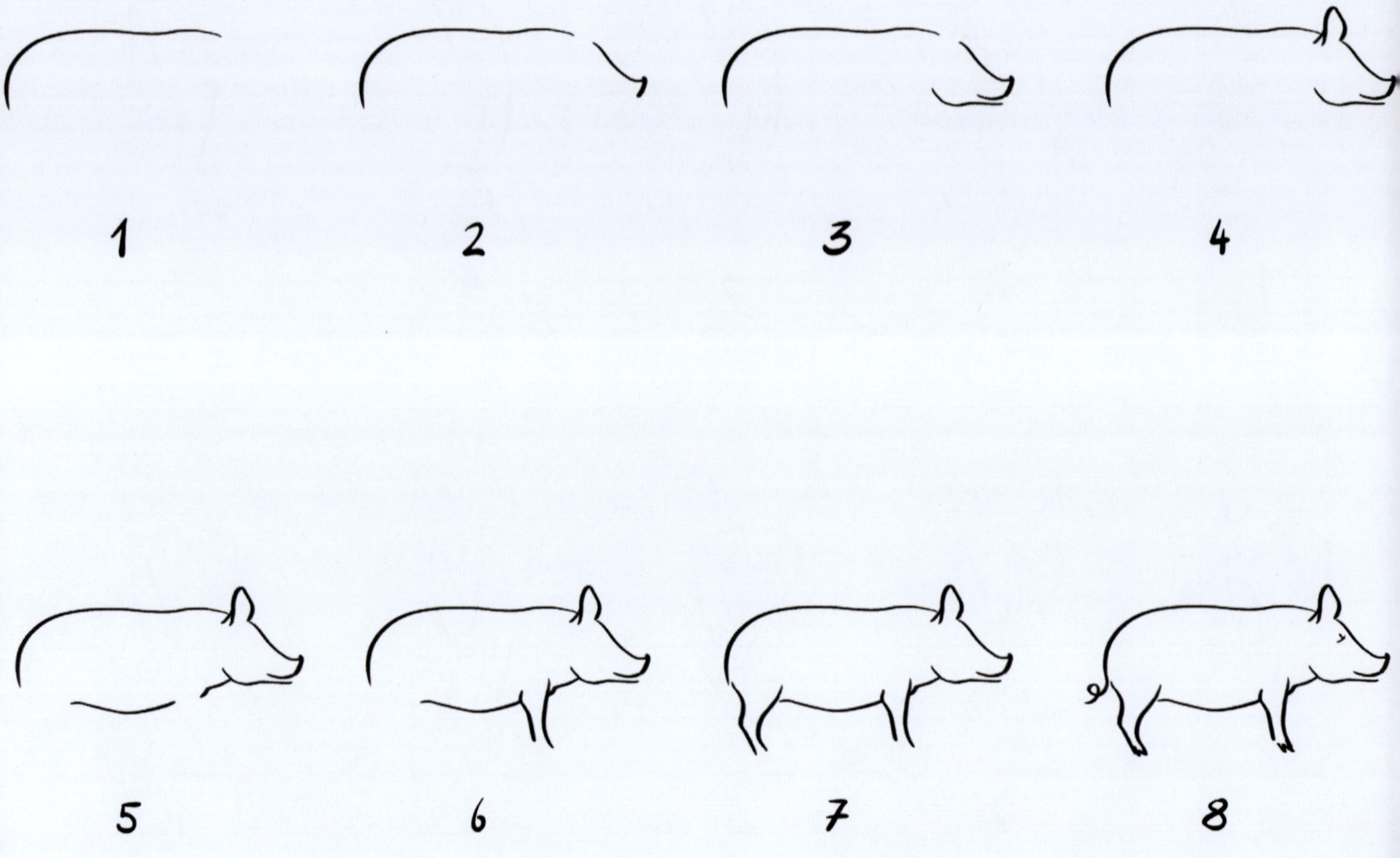

DAY 17

Tennis

DAY 18

Hammer

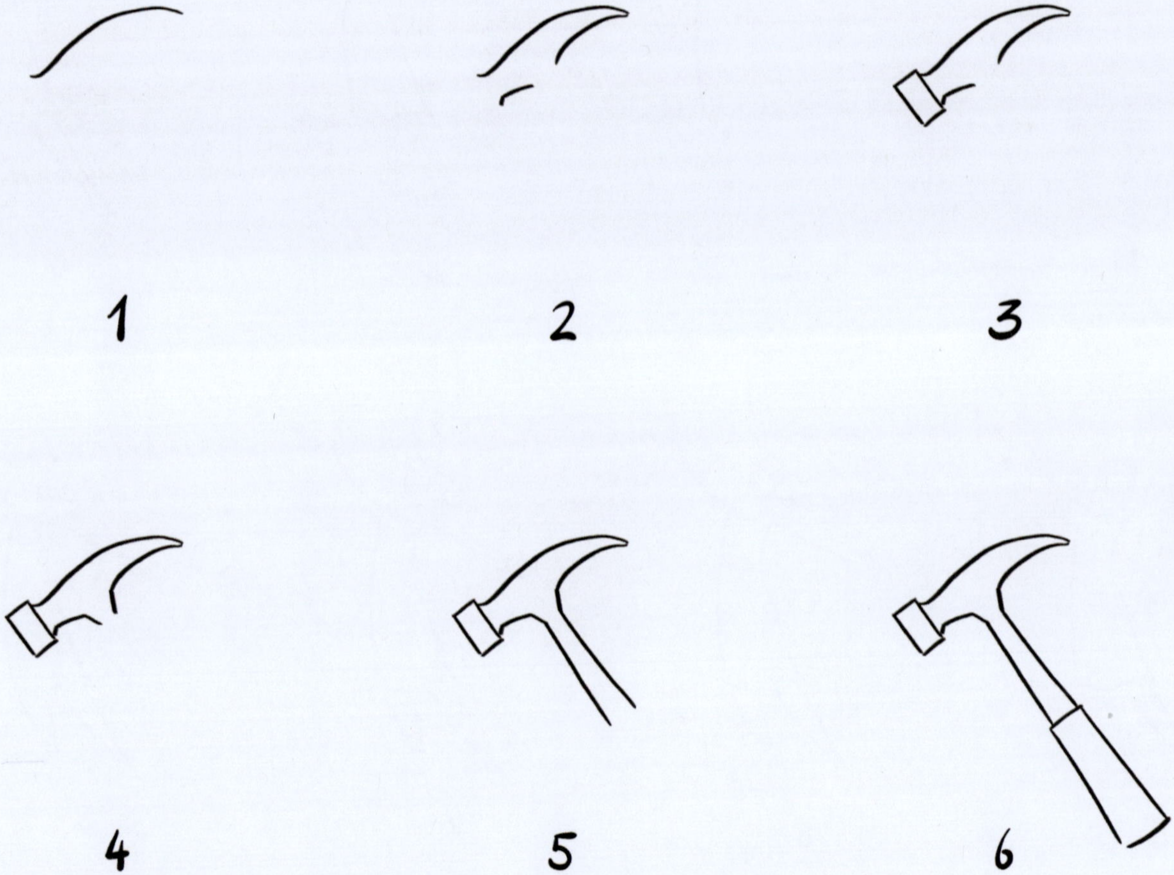

DAY 19

Kite

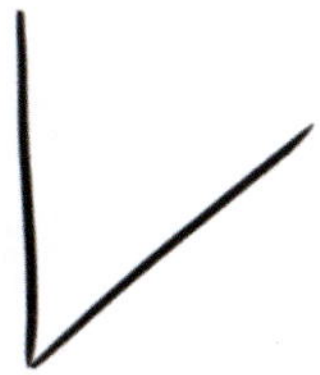

1

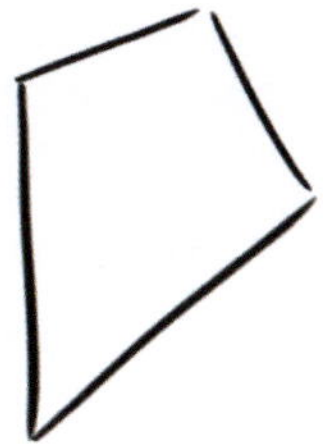

2

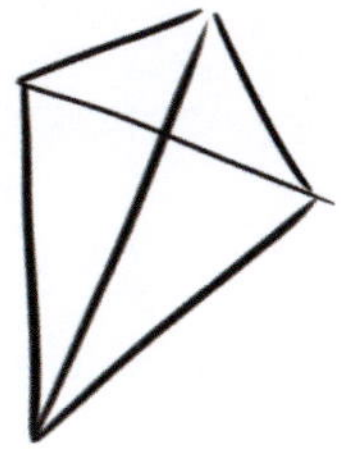

3

4

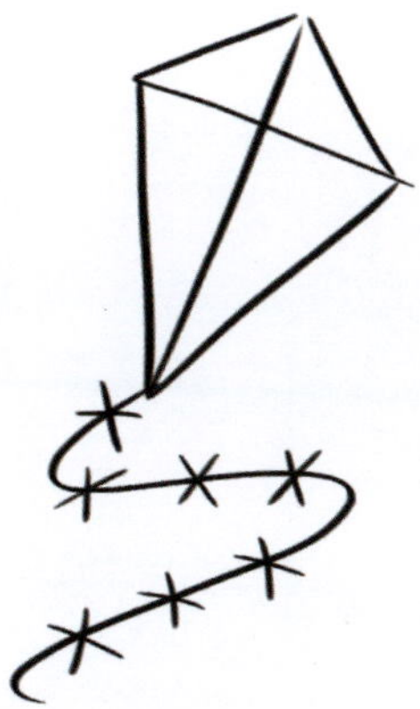

5

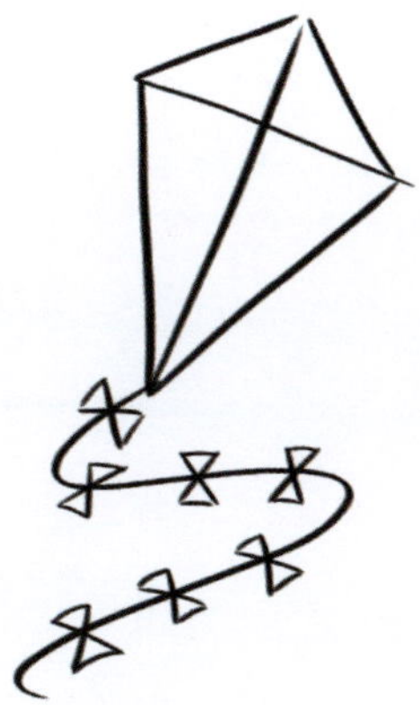

6

DAY 20

Fan

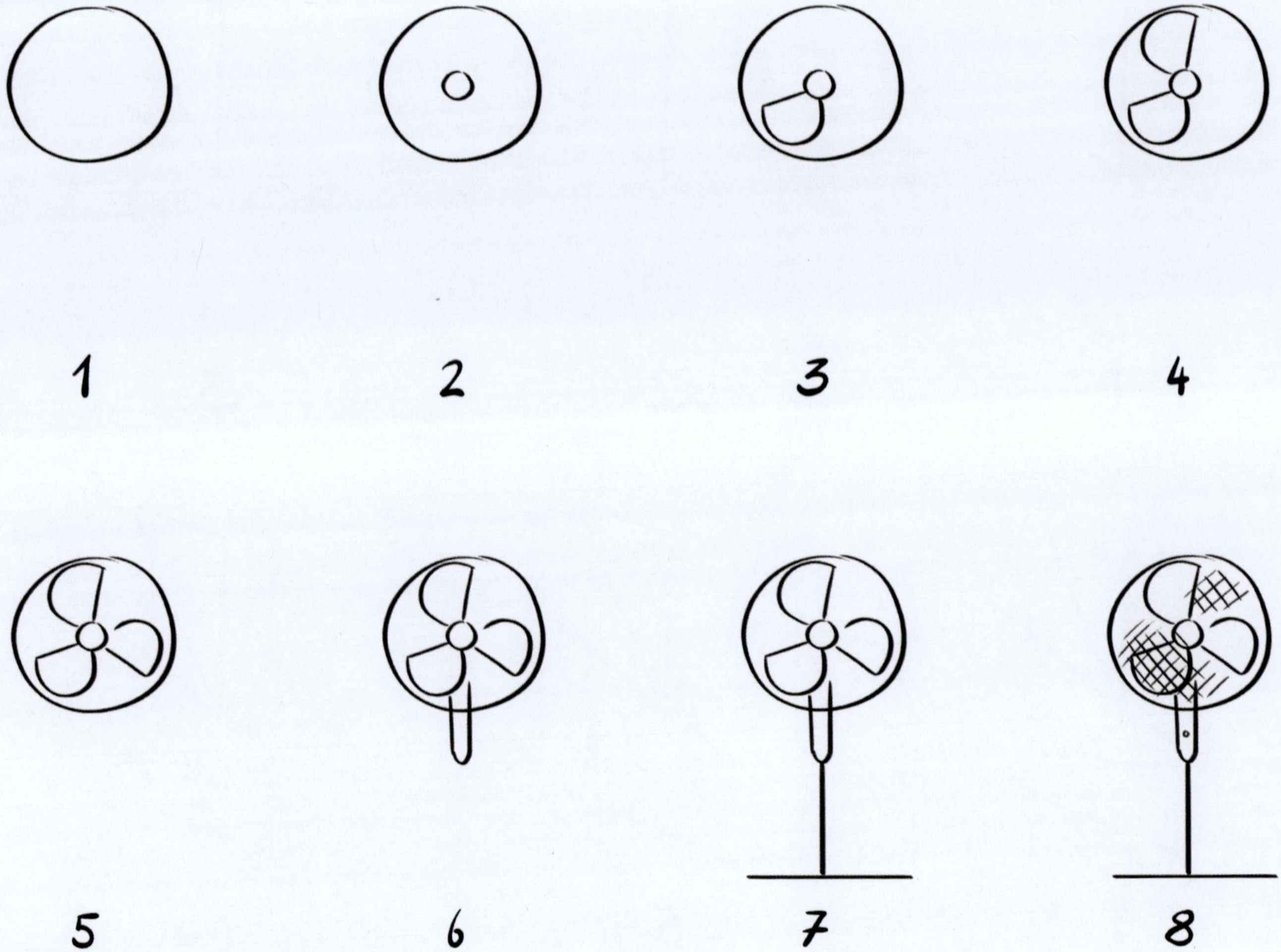

DAY 21

Crow

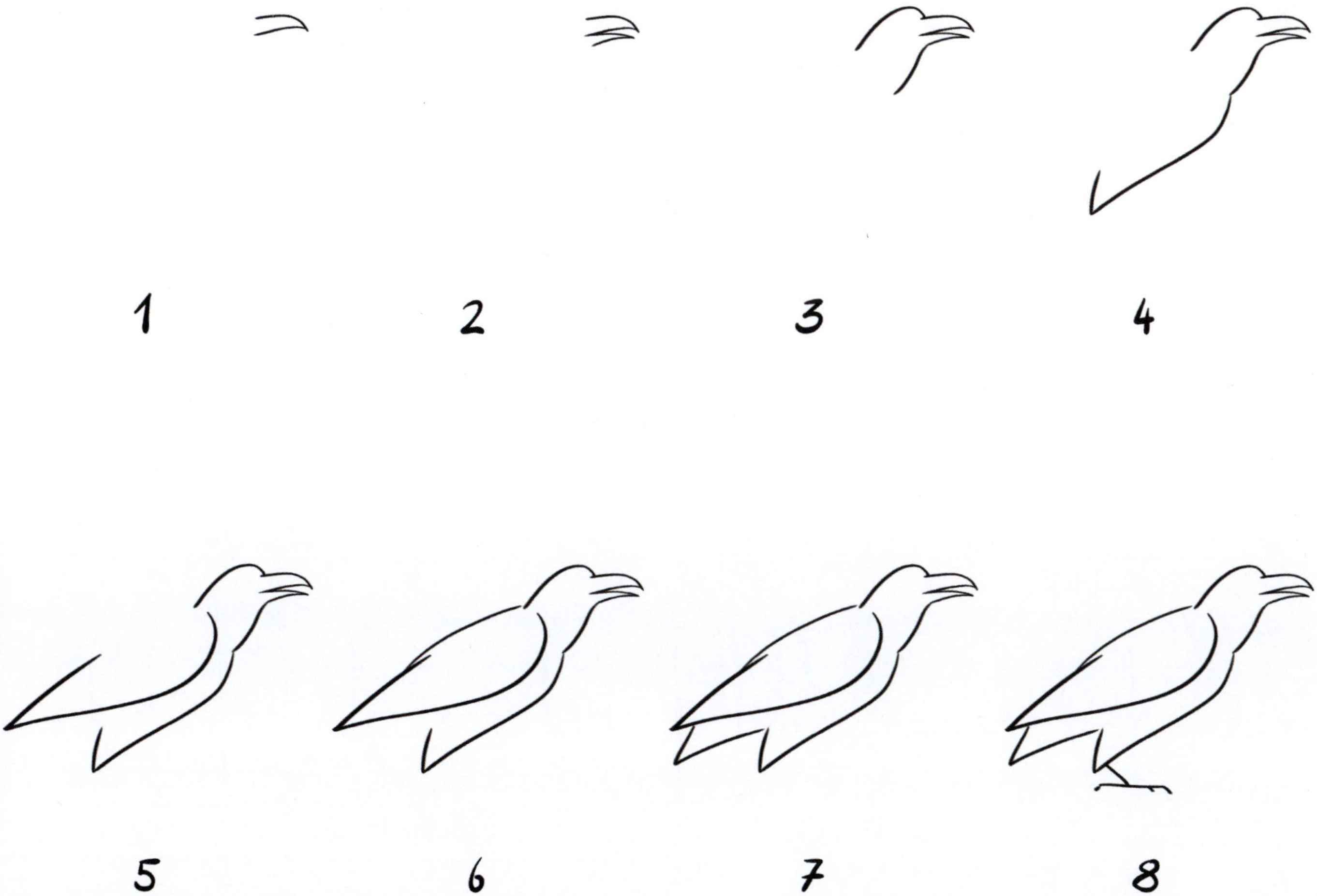

DAY 22

Pumpkin

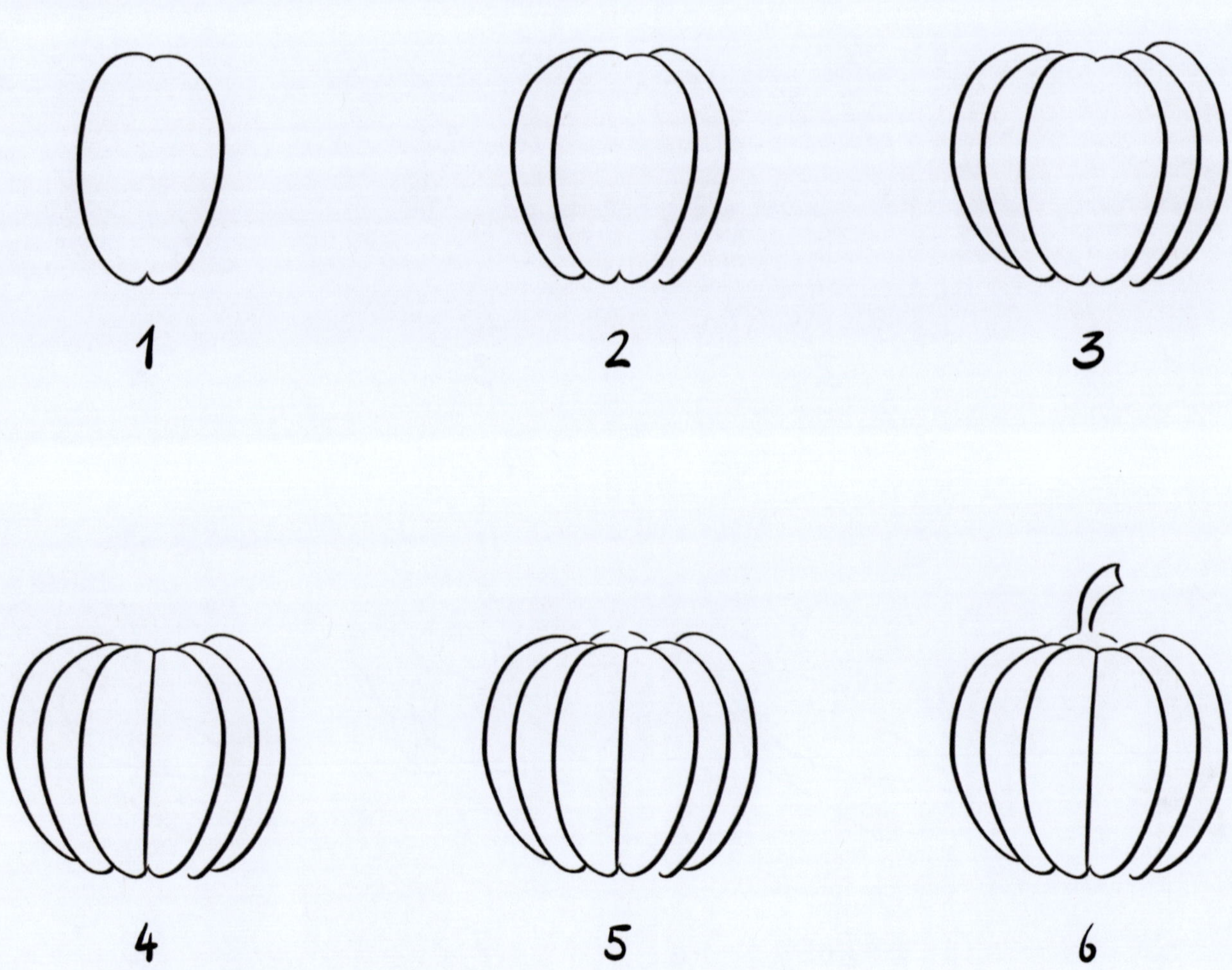

DAY 23

Climbing

1 2 3 4

5 6 7 8

DAY 24

Jar

1

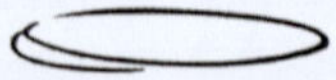

2

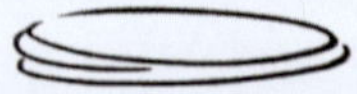

3

4

5

6

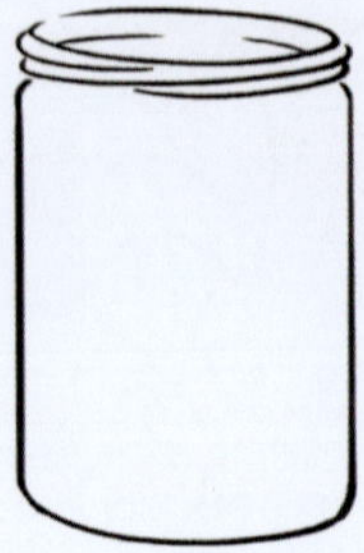

7

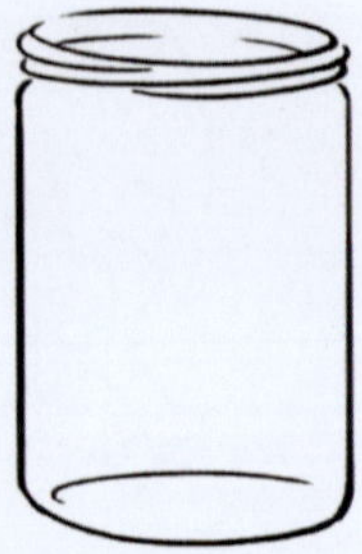

8

DAY 25

Lock

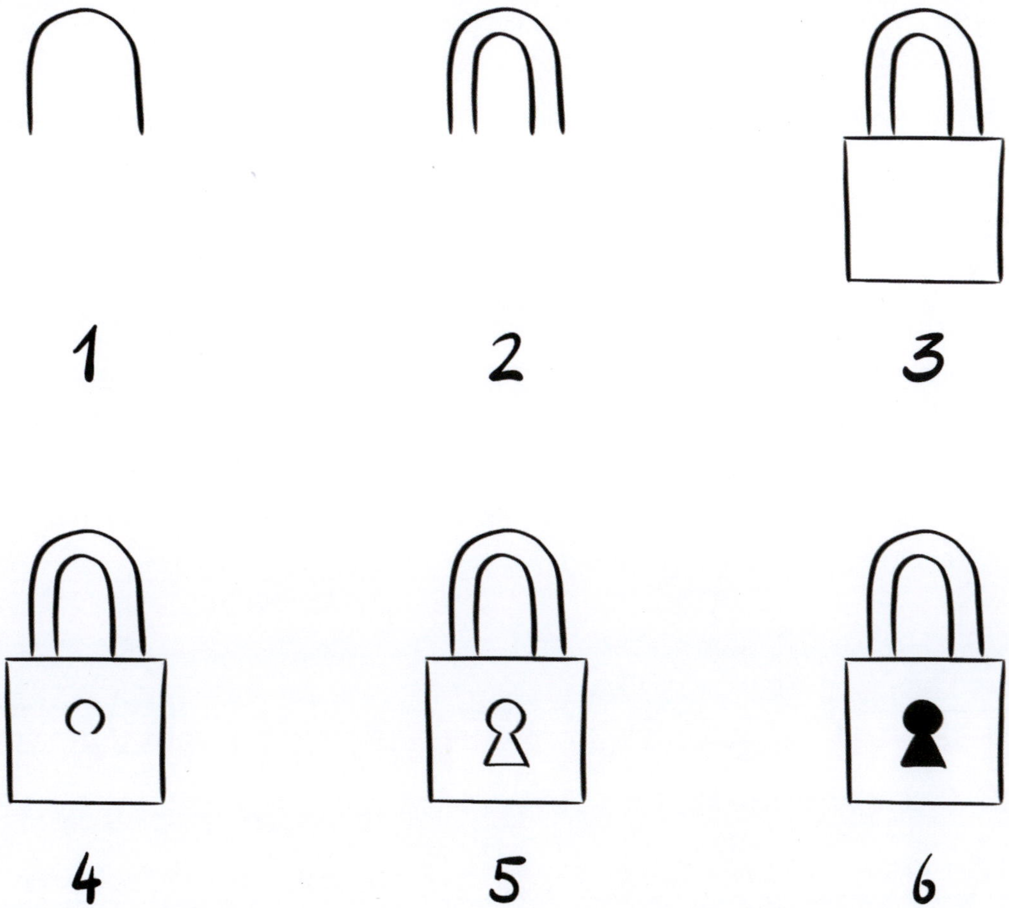

DAY 26

Key

1

2

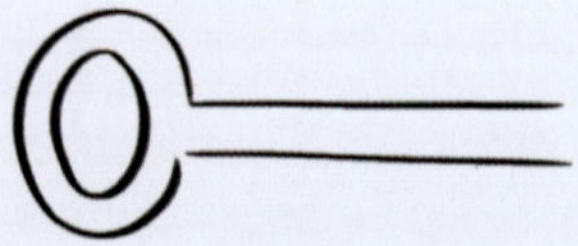

3

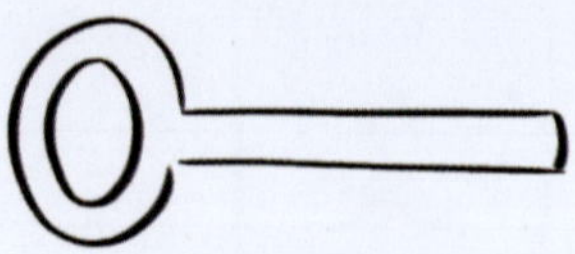

4

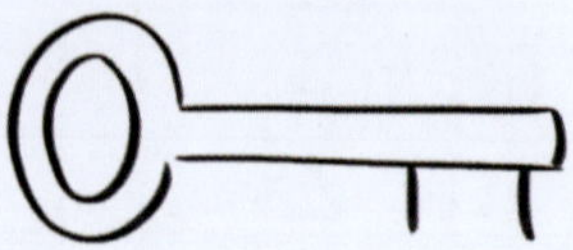

5

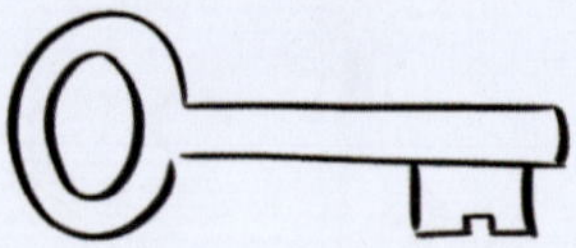

6

DAY 27

Hand in hand

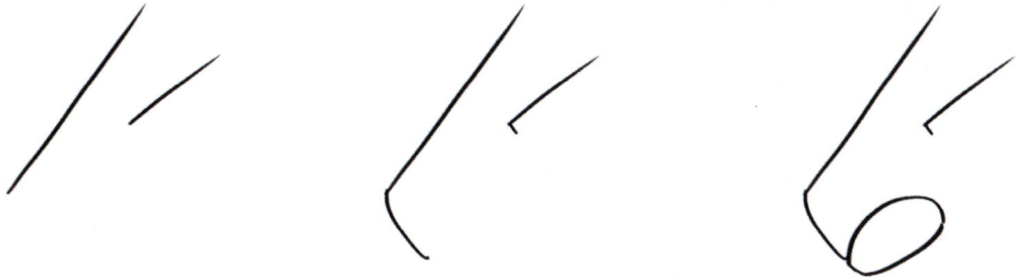

1 2 3

4 5 6 7

DAY 28

Espresso

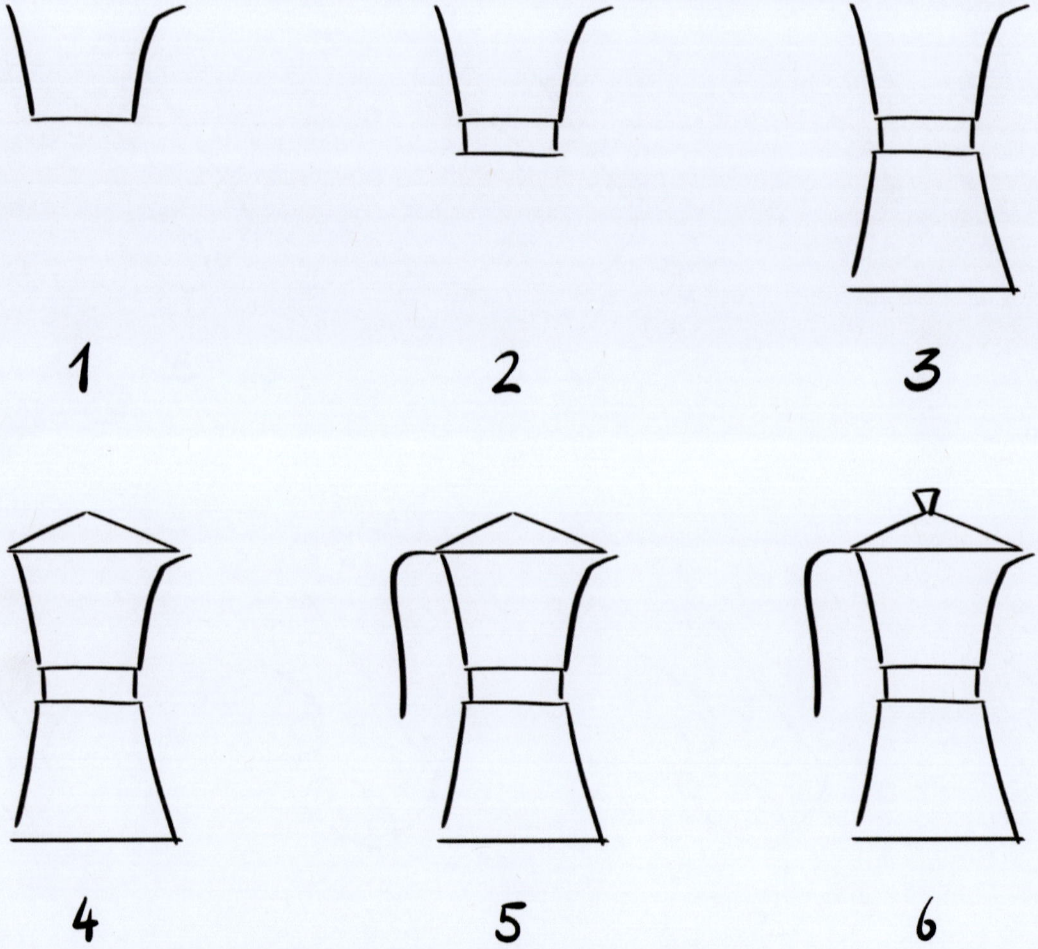

DAY 29

Top hat

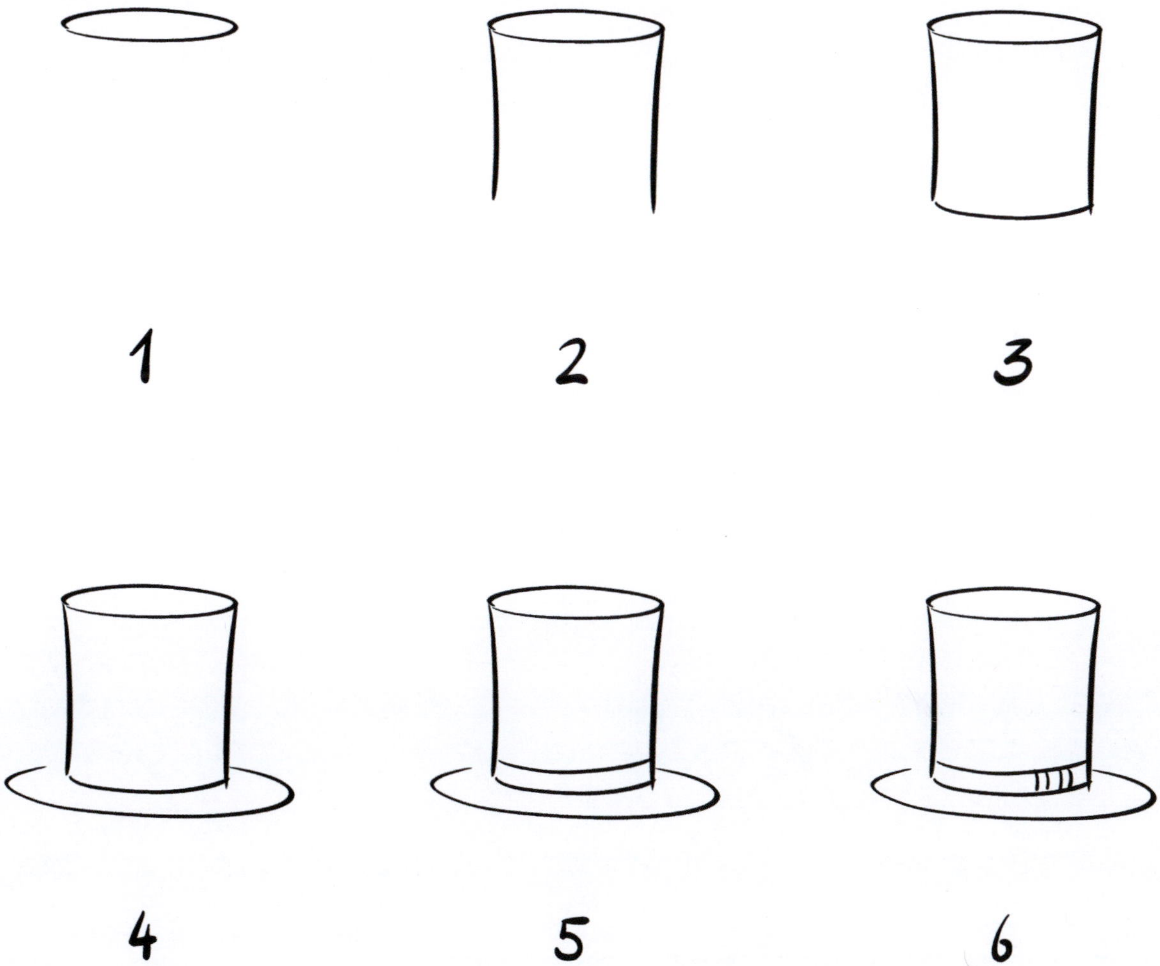

DAY 30

Matches

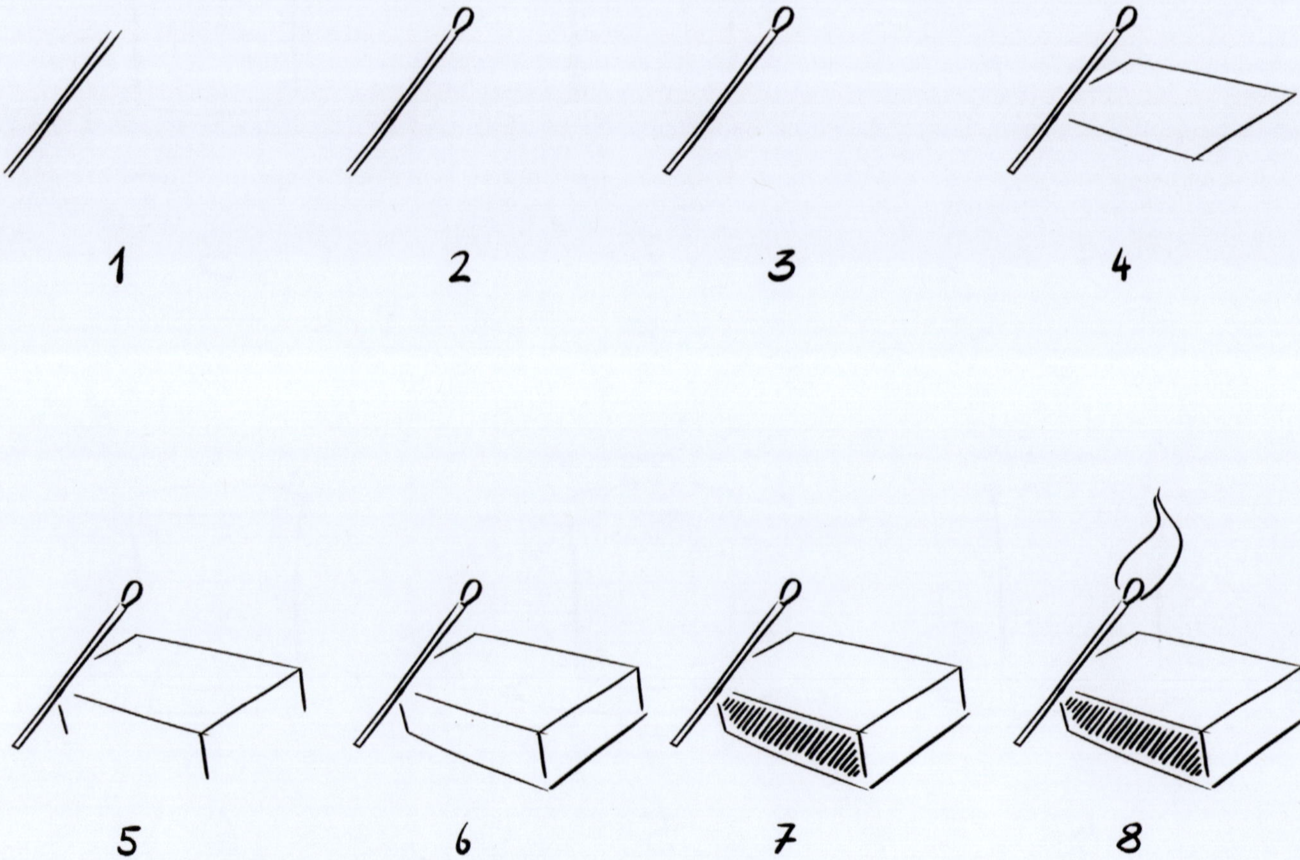

DAY 31

Tomato

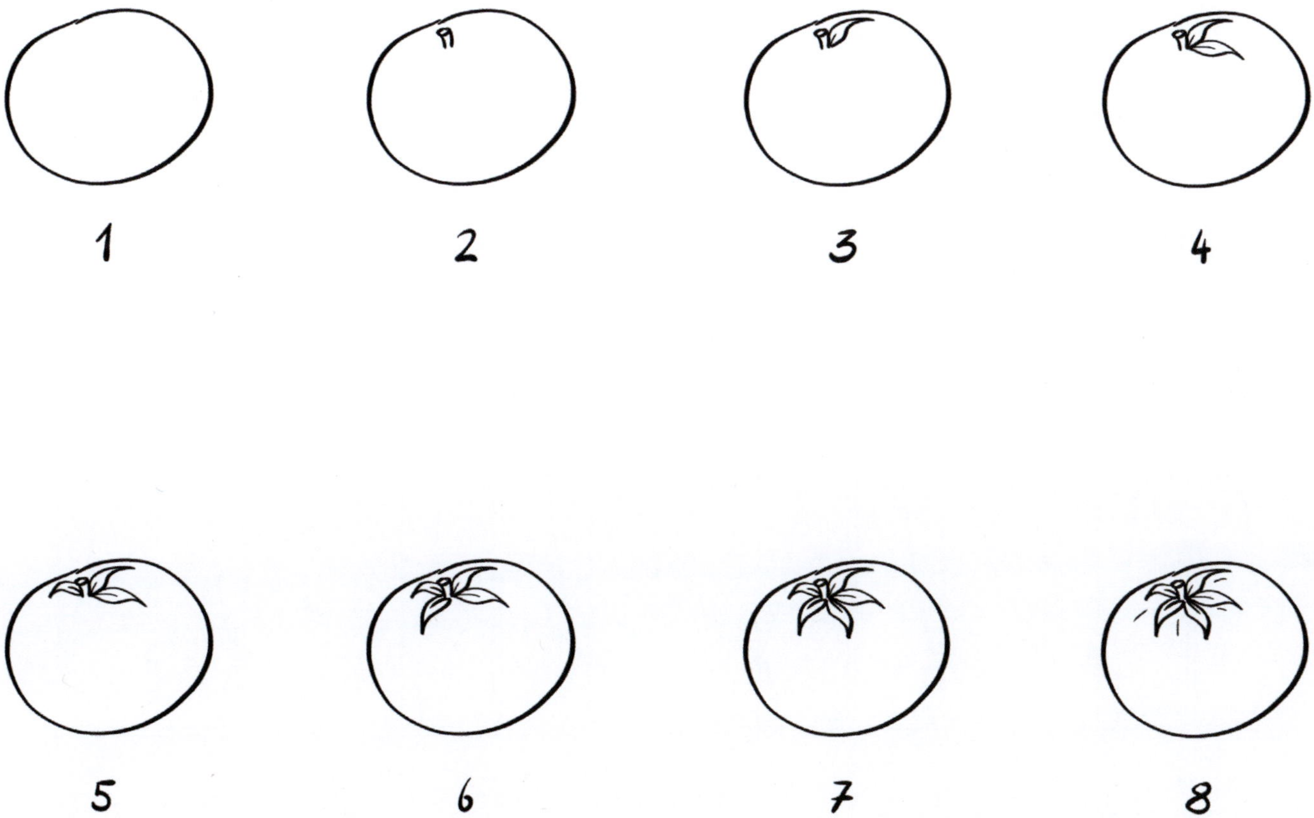

DAY 32

Window

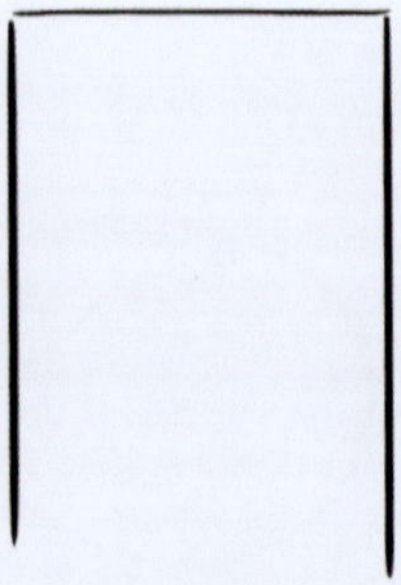

1

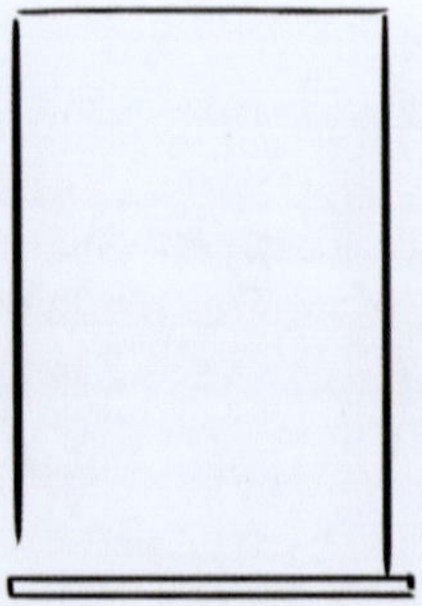

2

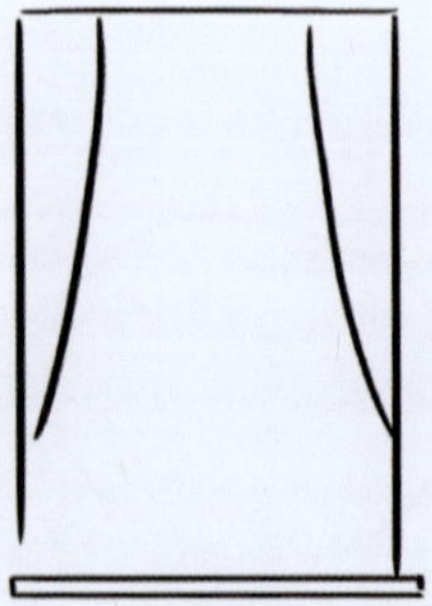

3

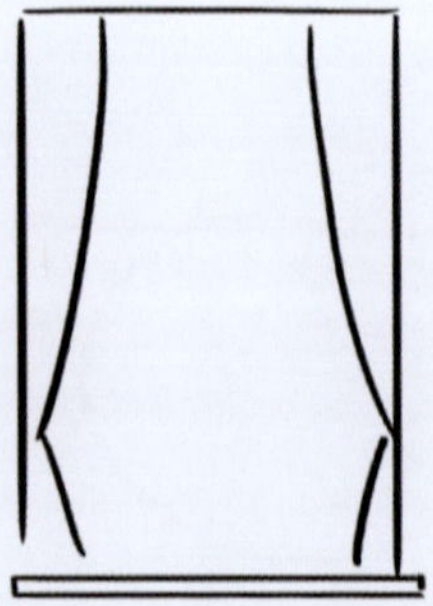

4

5

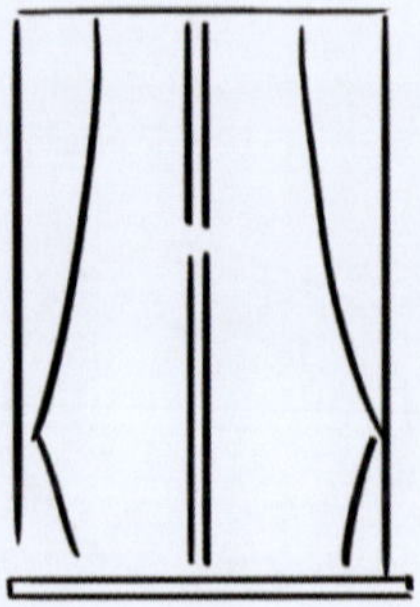

6

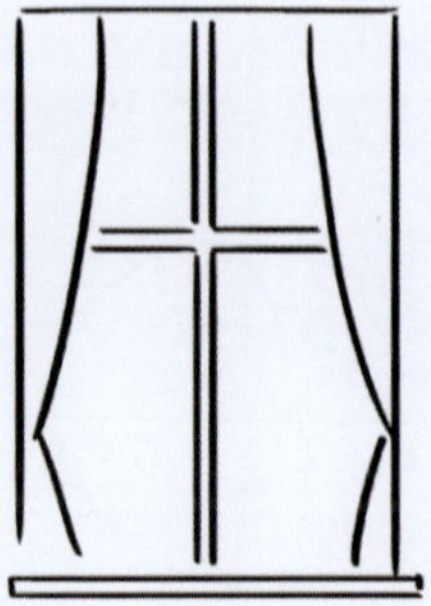

7

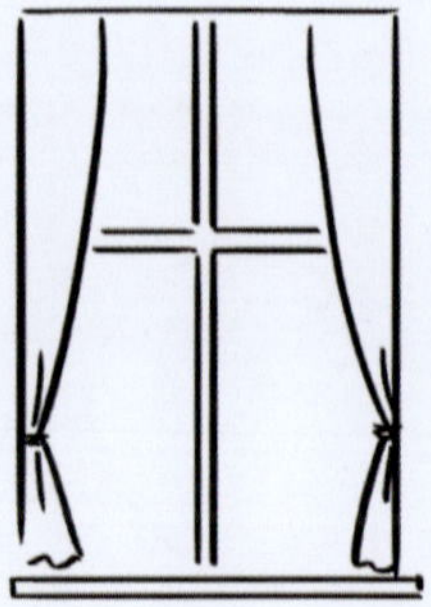

8

DAY 33

Newspaper

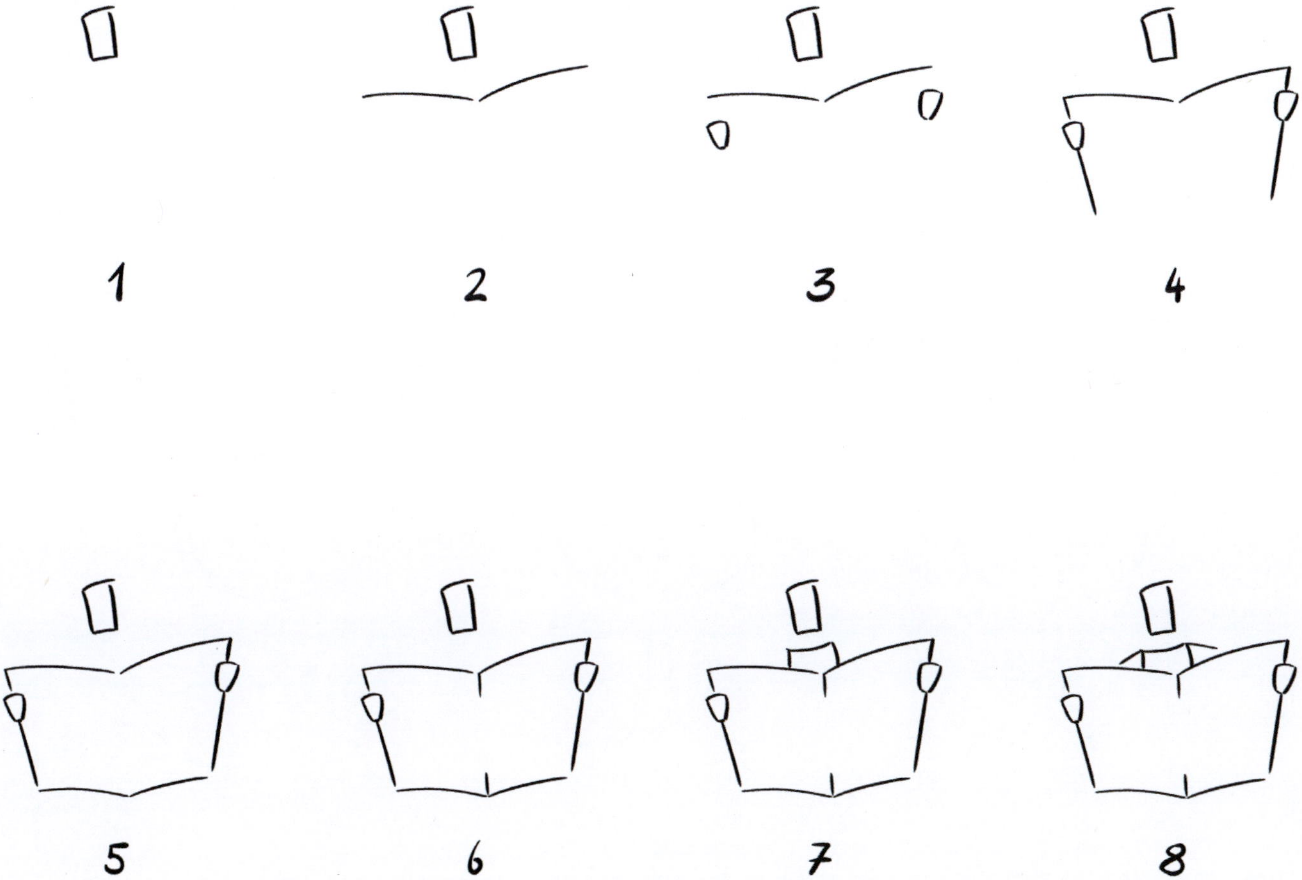

DAY 34

Wine

1

2

3

4

5

6

DAY 35

Drill

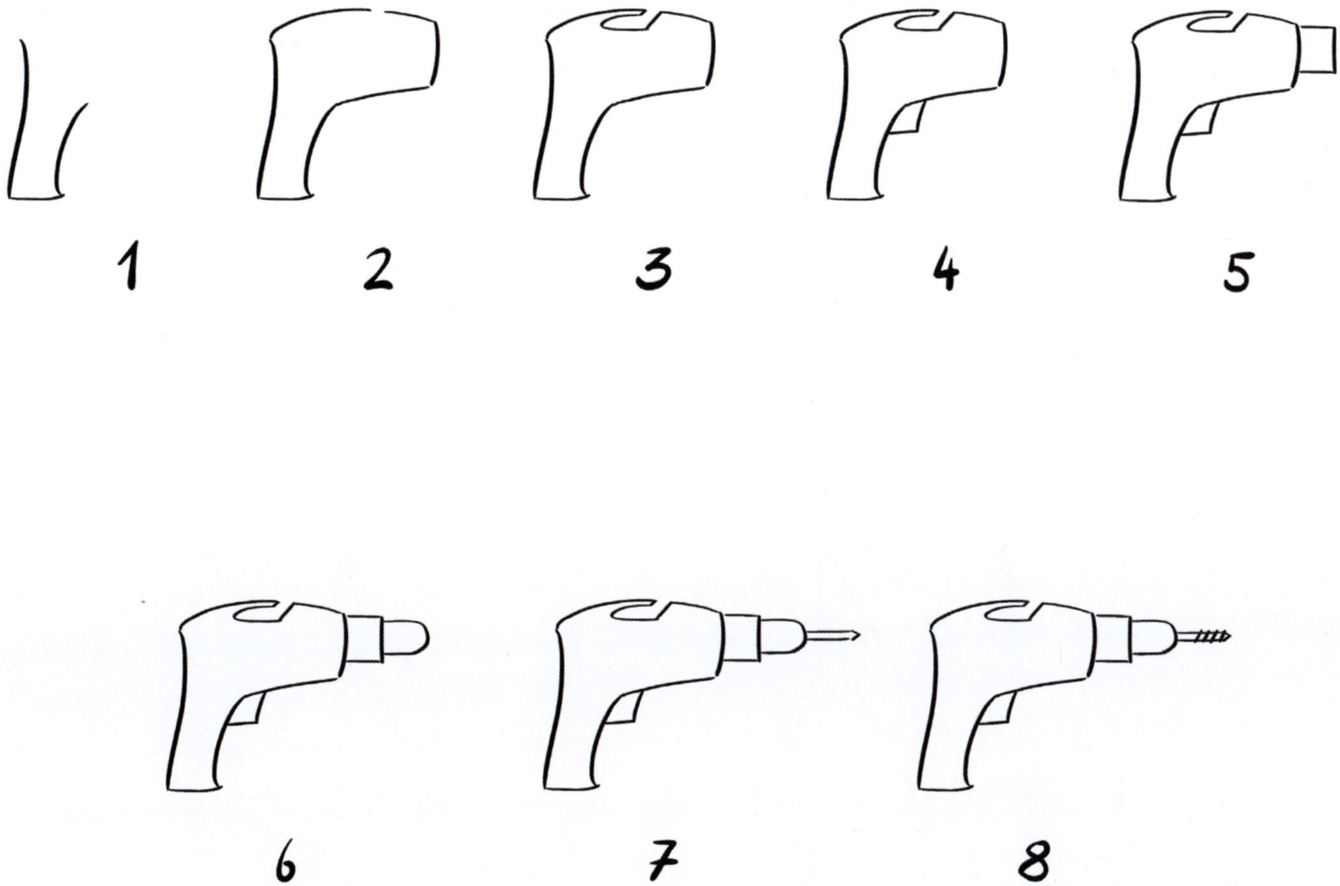

DAY 36

Book

1

2

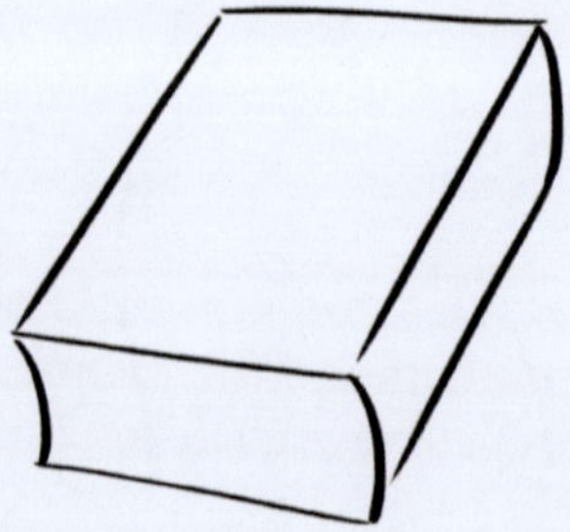

3

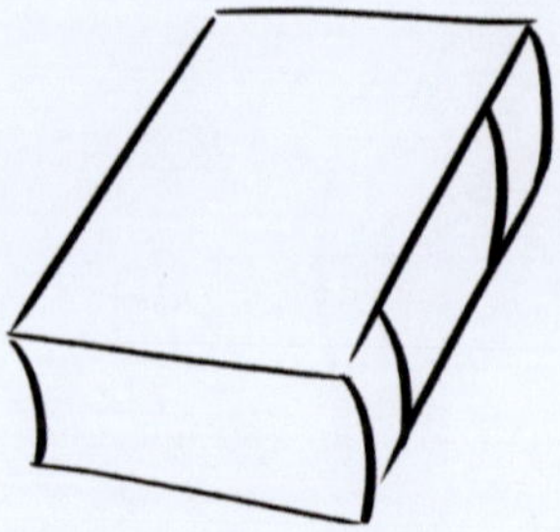

4

5

DAY 37

Bread

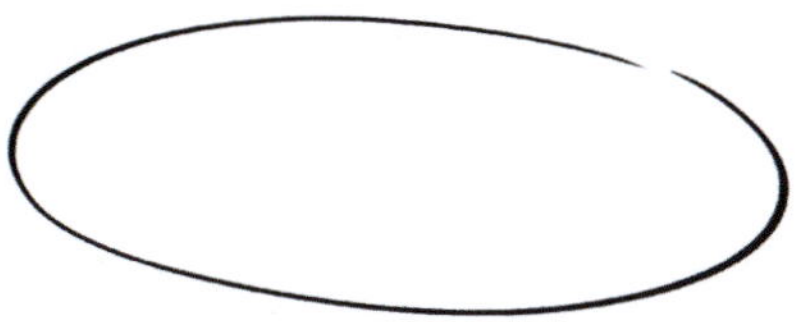

1

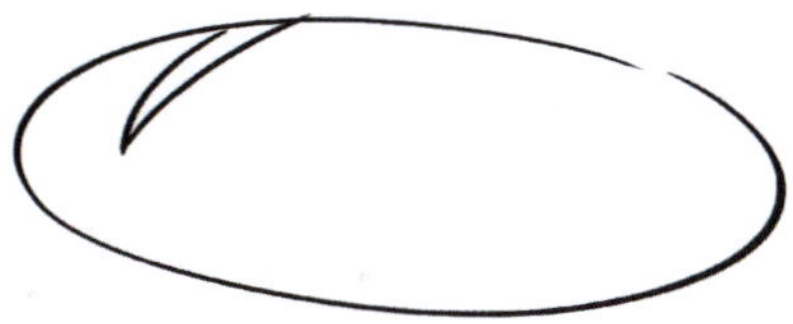

2

3

4

5

DAY 38

Meditation

DAY 39

Money

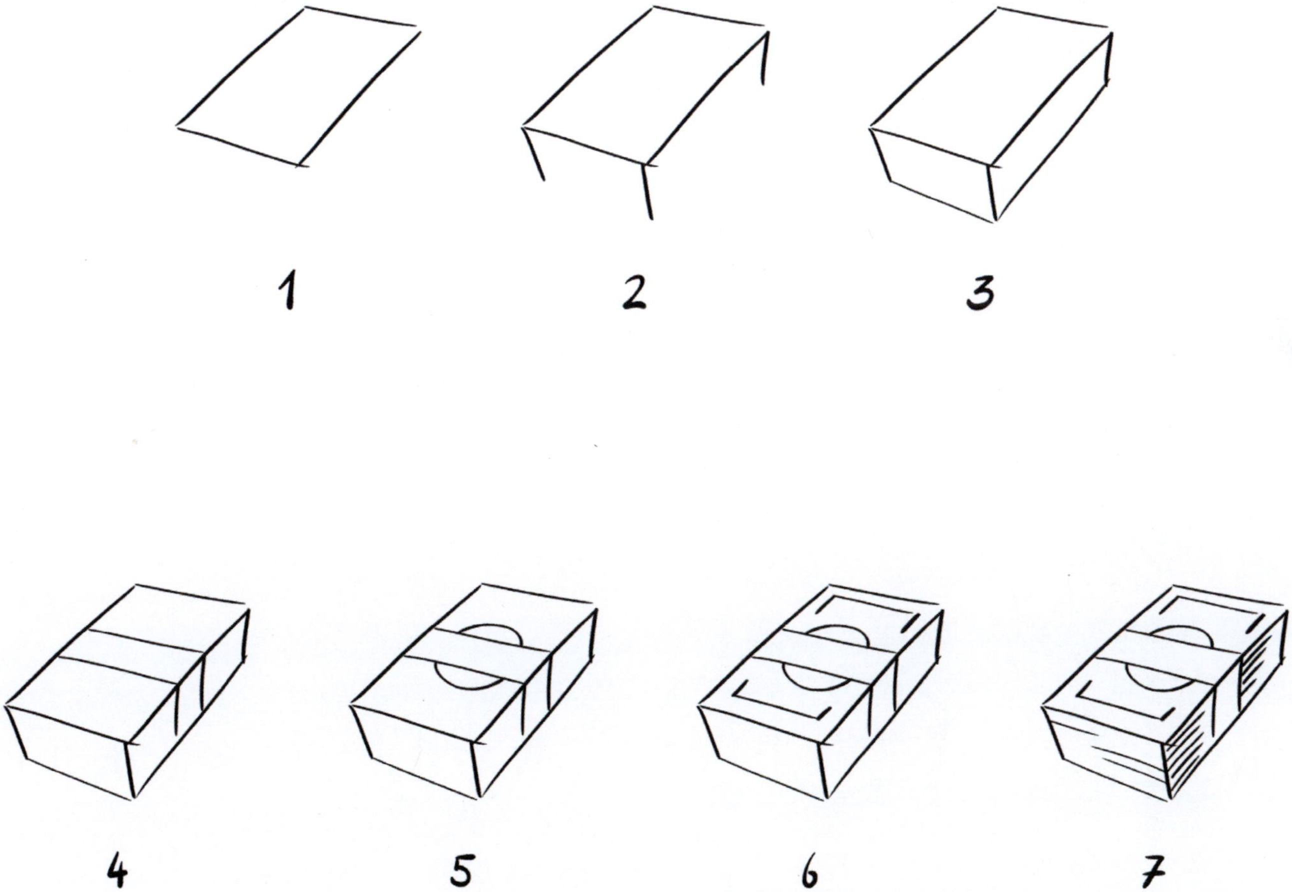

DAY 40

Wristwatch

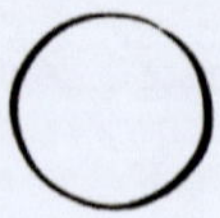

1

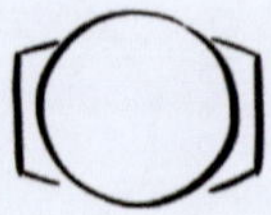

2

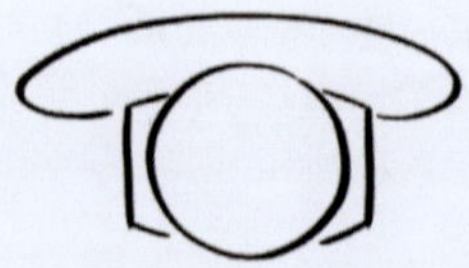

3

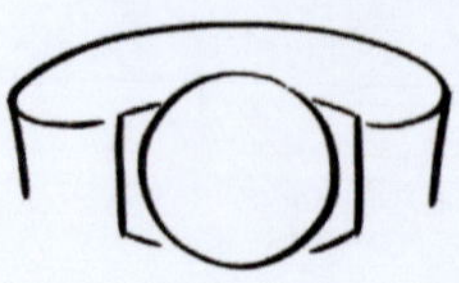

4

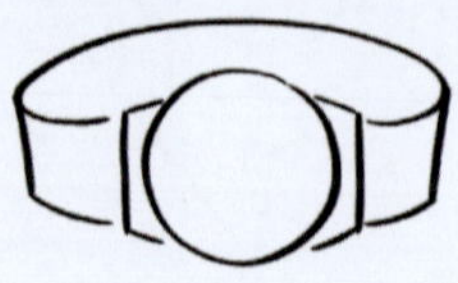

5

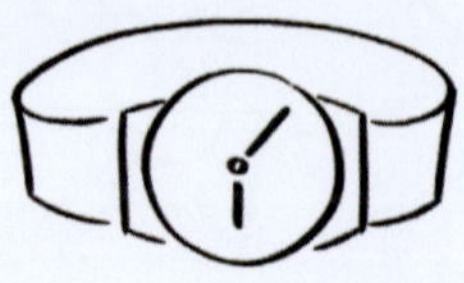

6

7

DAY 41

Compasses

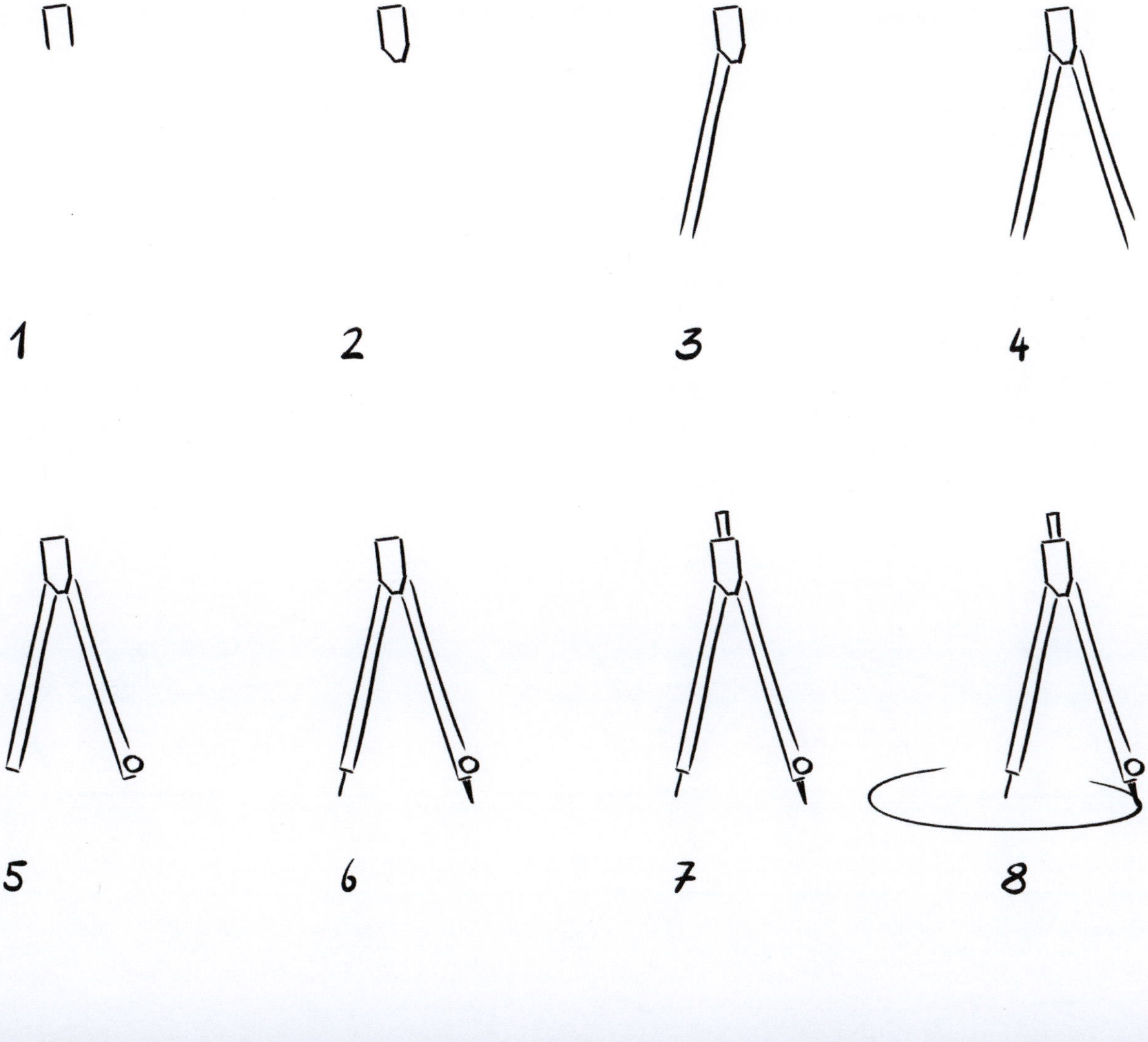

DAY 42

Paper boat

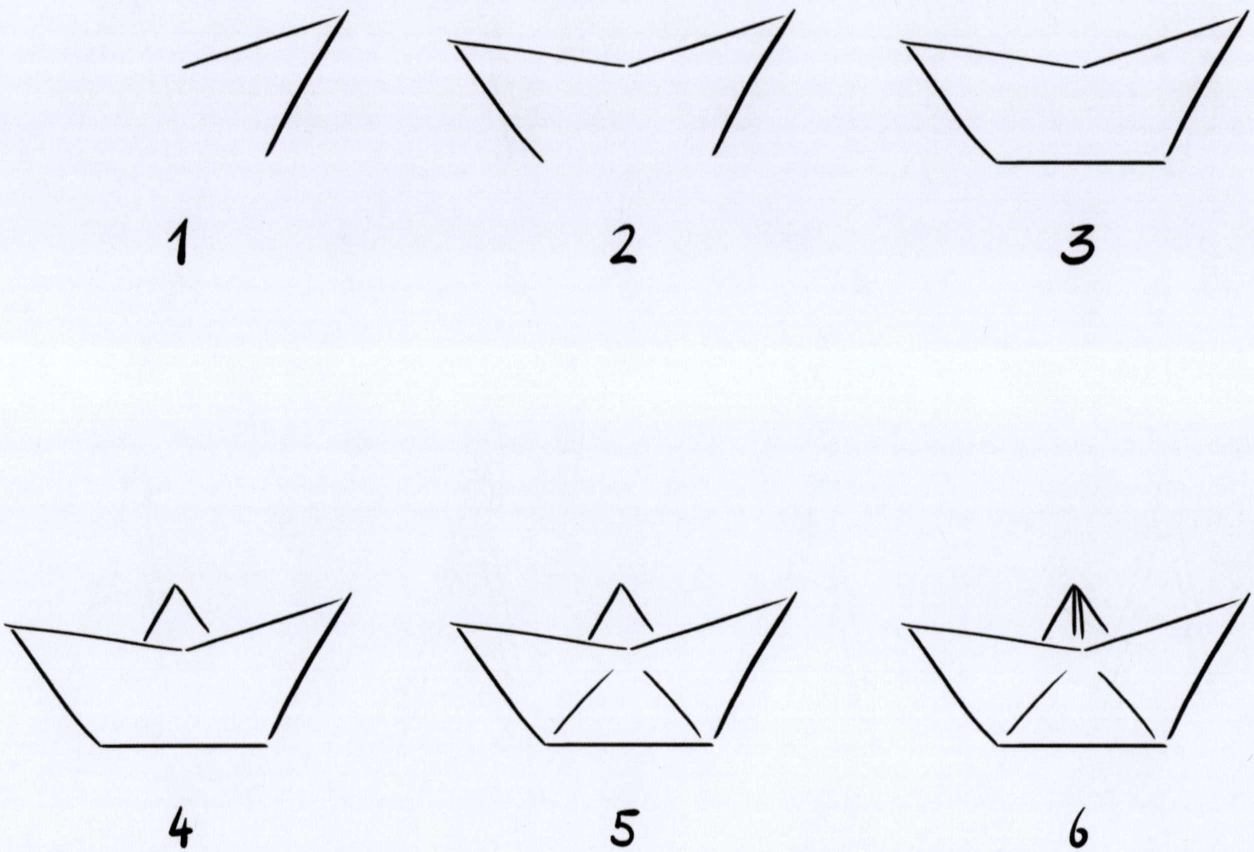

DAY 43

Climbing stairs

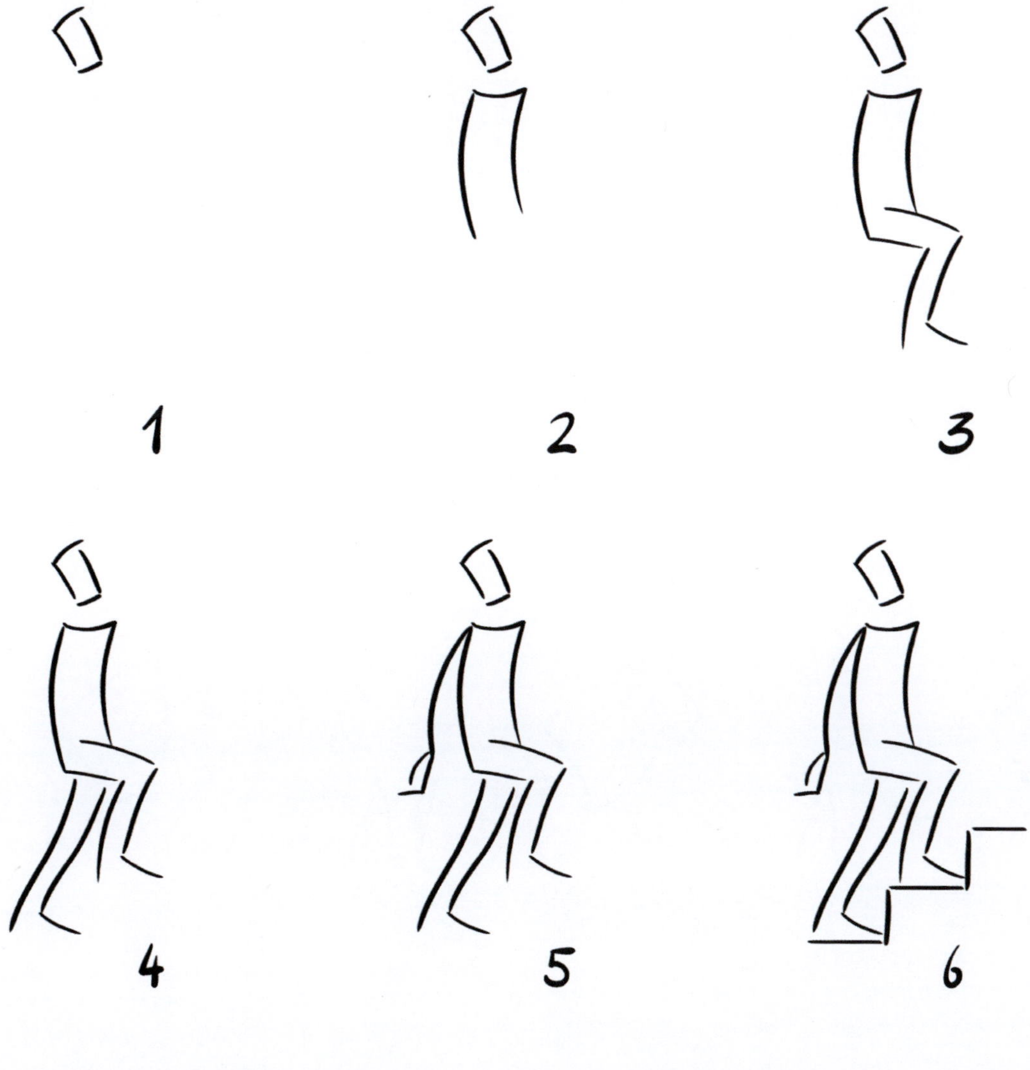

DAY 44

Lion

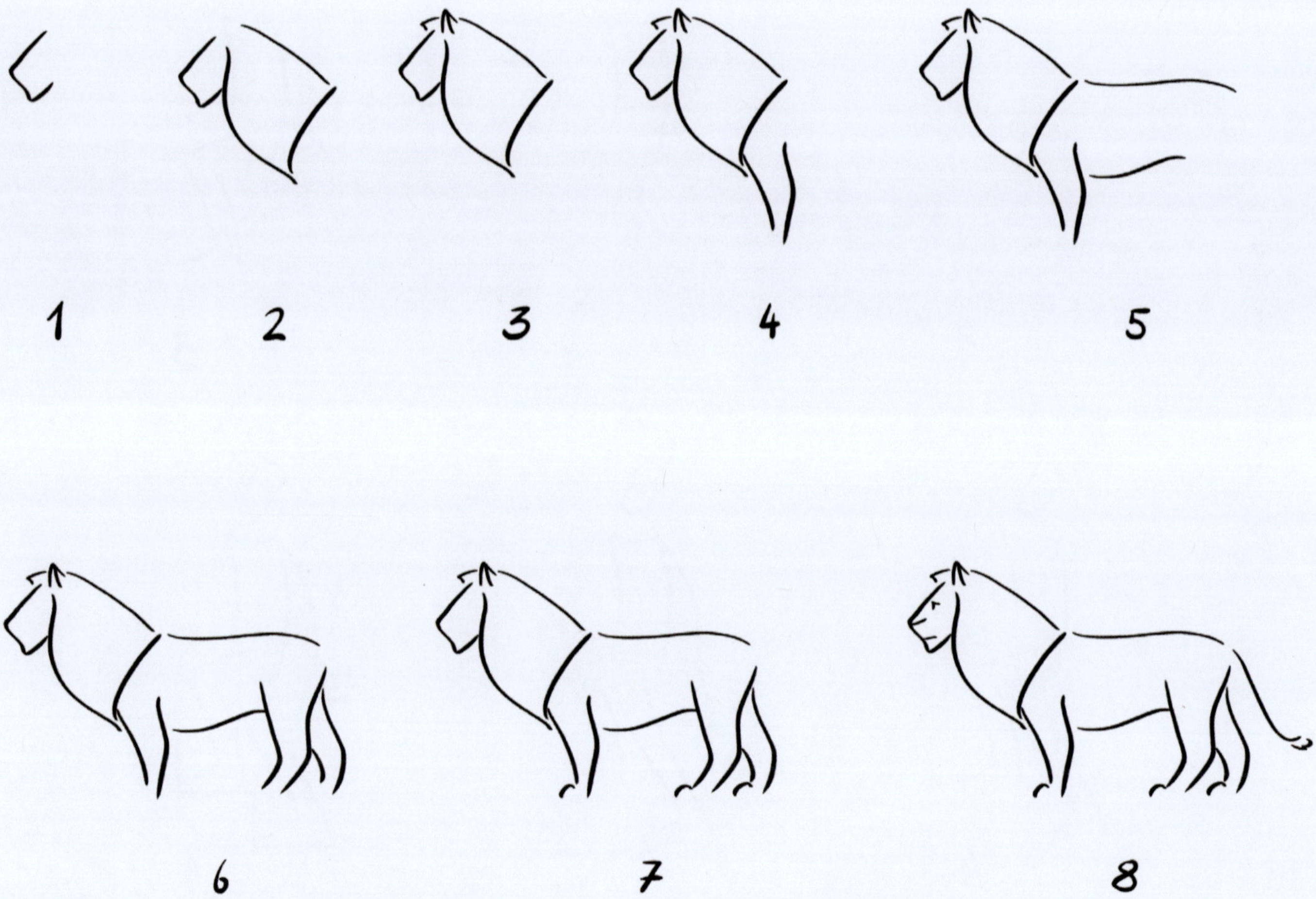

DAY 45

Washing machine

1

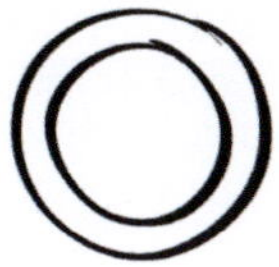

2

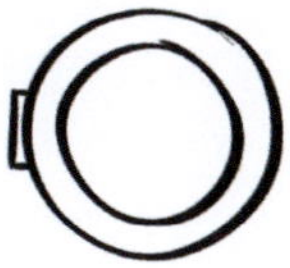

3

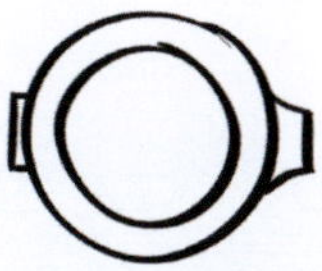

4

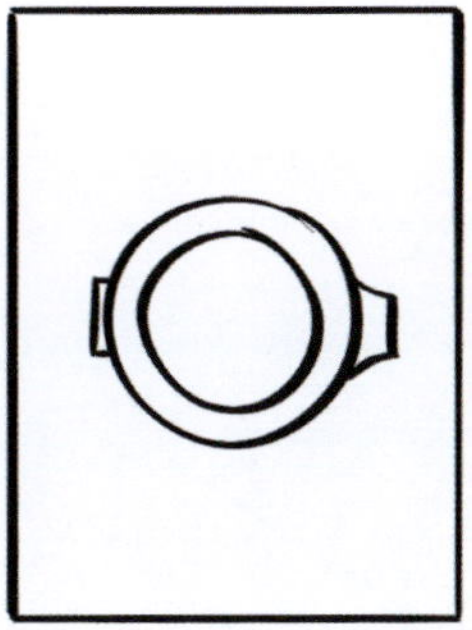

5

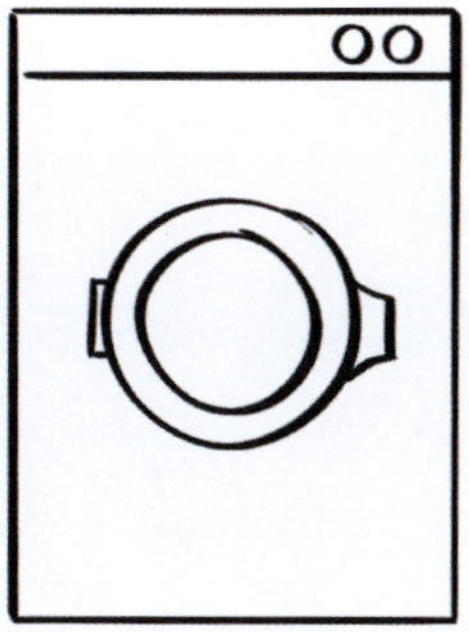

6

DAY 46

Sled

1

2

3

4

5

6

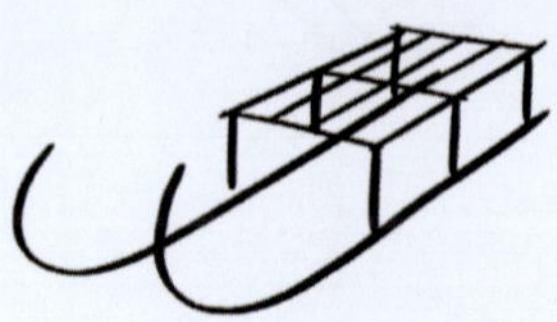

7

DAY 47

Christmas tree

1

2

3

4

5

6

DAY 48

Shooting star

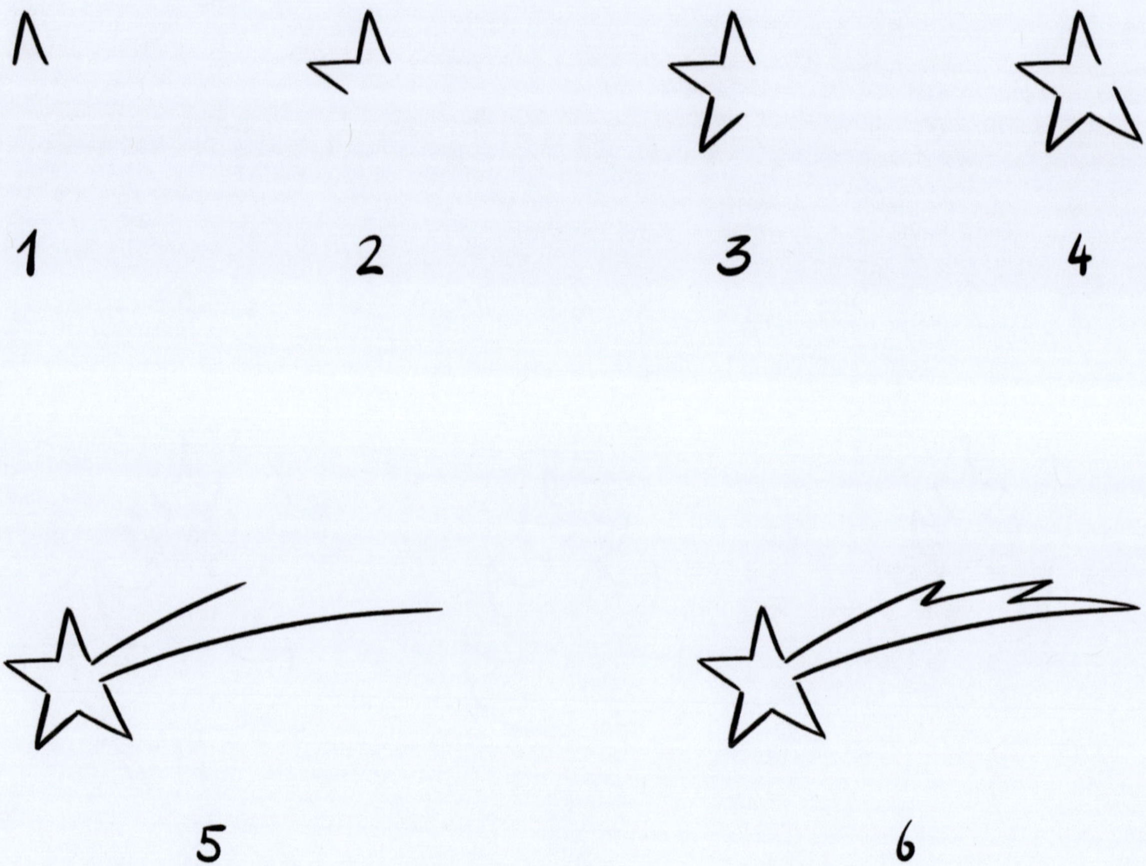

DAY 49

Snowflake

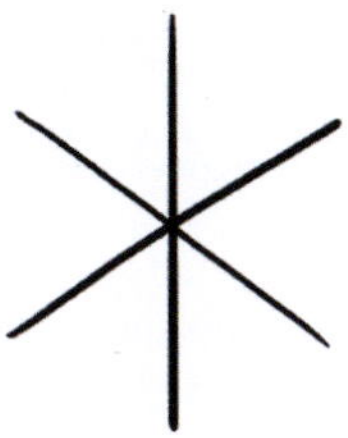

1

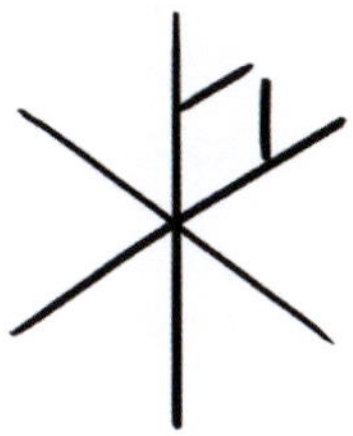

2

3

4

5

6

7

8

DAY 50

Ice skating

1

2

3

4

5

6

7

8

DAY 51

Holiday candle

1

2

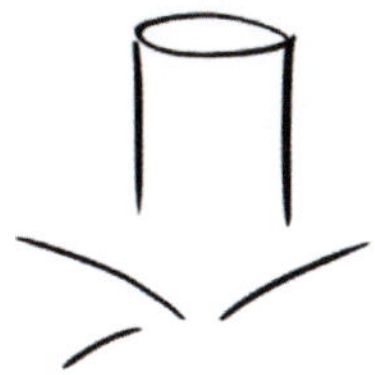

3

4

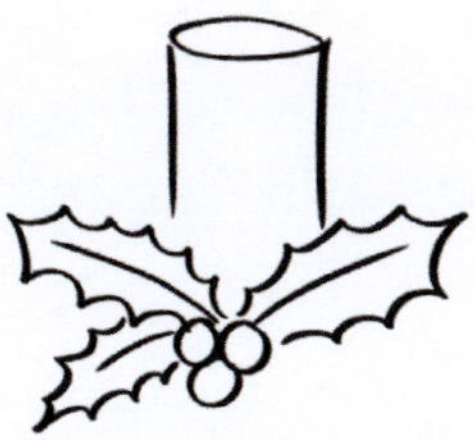

5

6

7

8

DAY 52

Santa

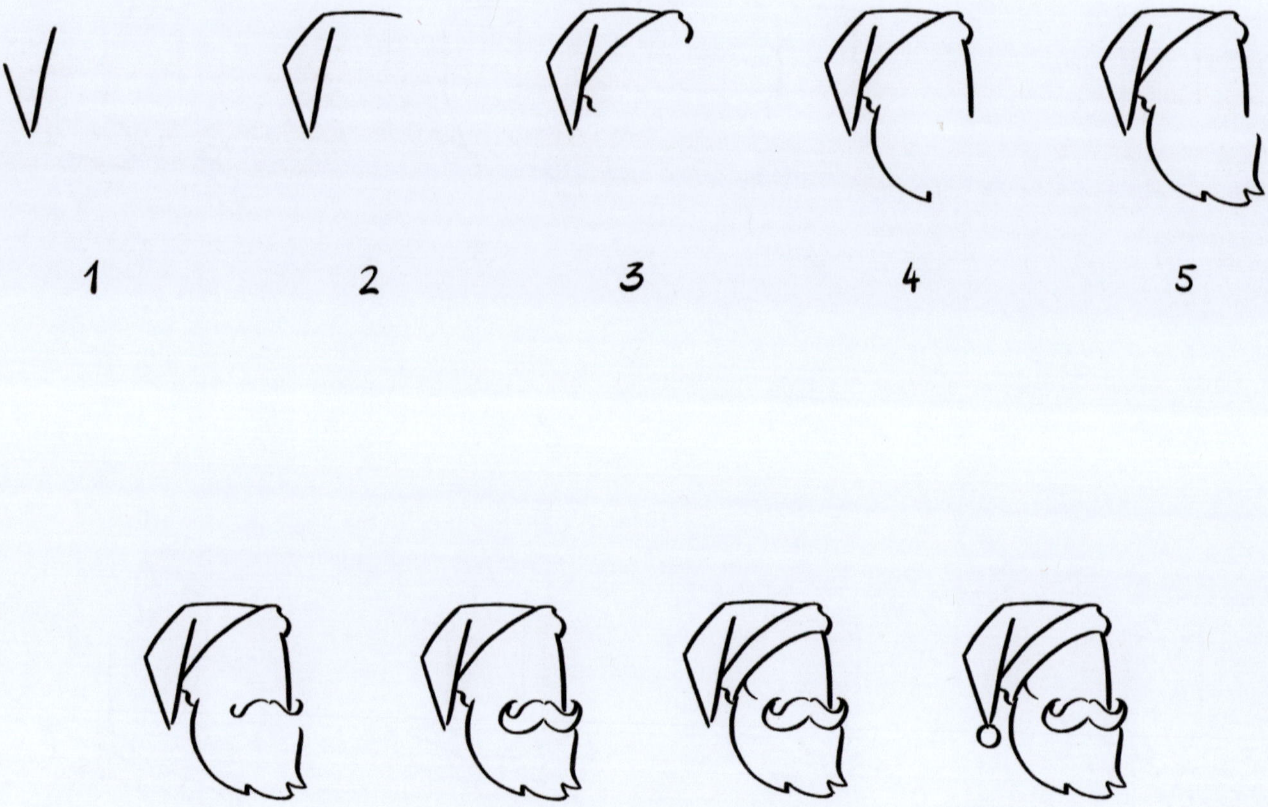

DAY 53

Snowman

1

2

3

4

5

6

7

8

DAY 54

Rocking horse

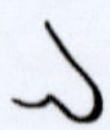

1

2

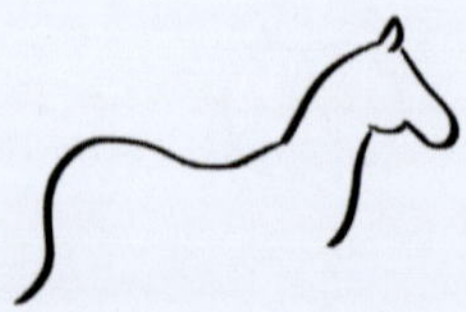

3

4

5

6

7

8

DAY 55

Christmas bauble

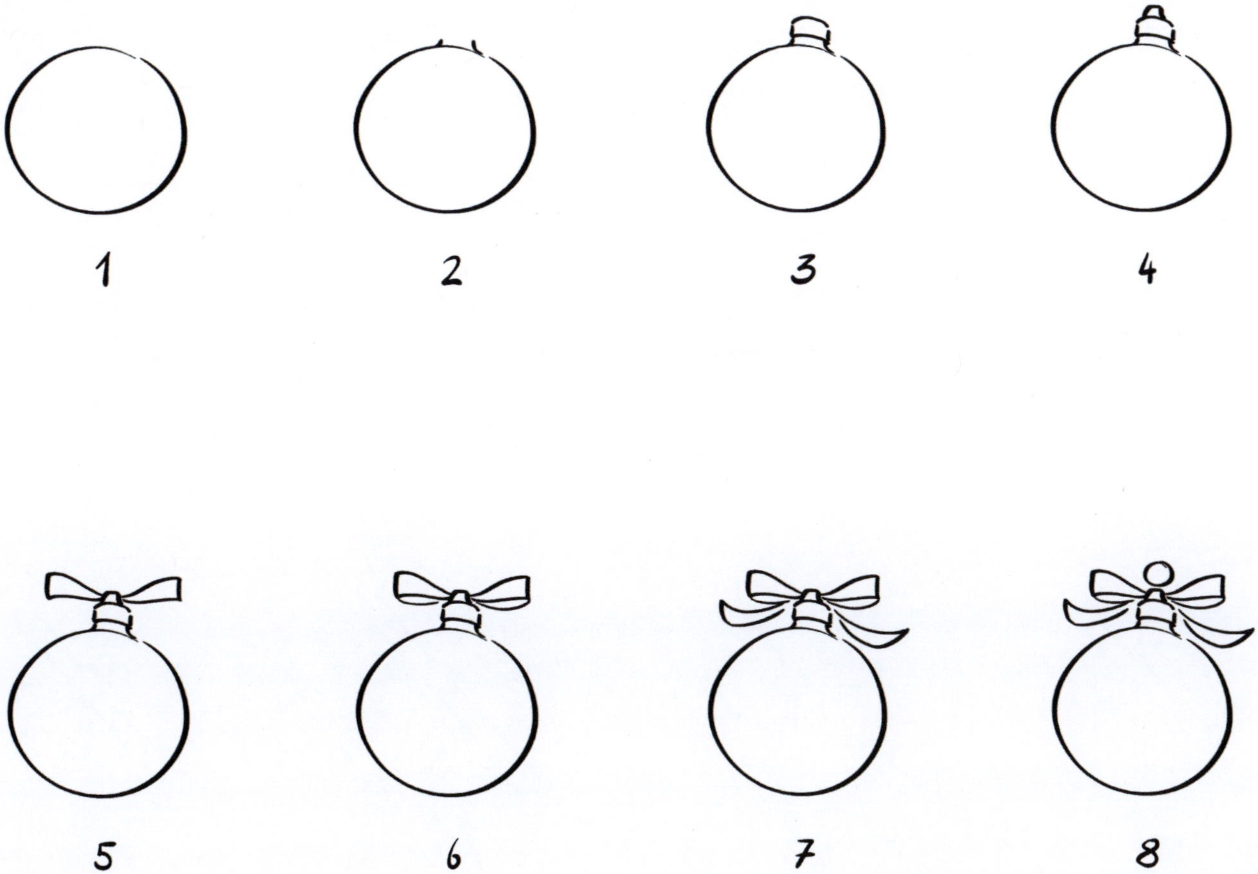

DAY 56

Candy

1

2

3

4

5

6

7

8

DAY 57

St. Nicholas

1 2 3 4 5

6 7 8 9 10

DAY 58

Reindeer

1

2

3

4

5

6

7

8

9

DAY 59

Christmas stocking

1

2

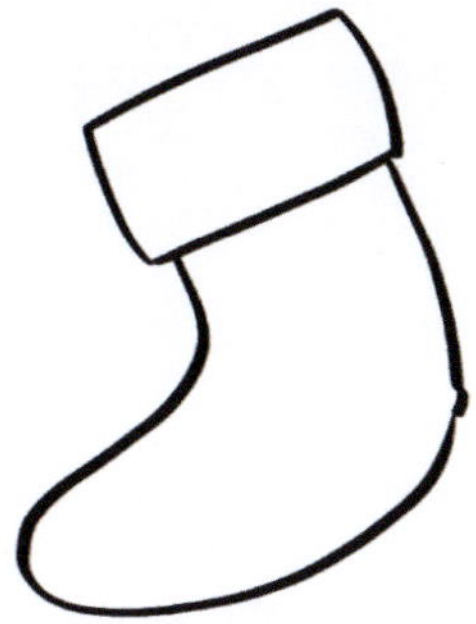

3

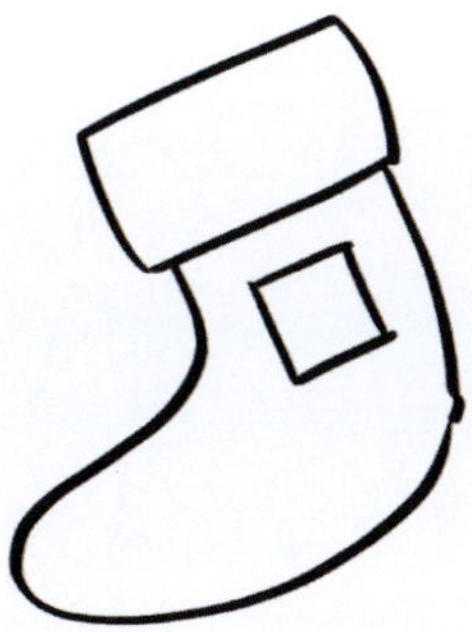

4

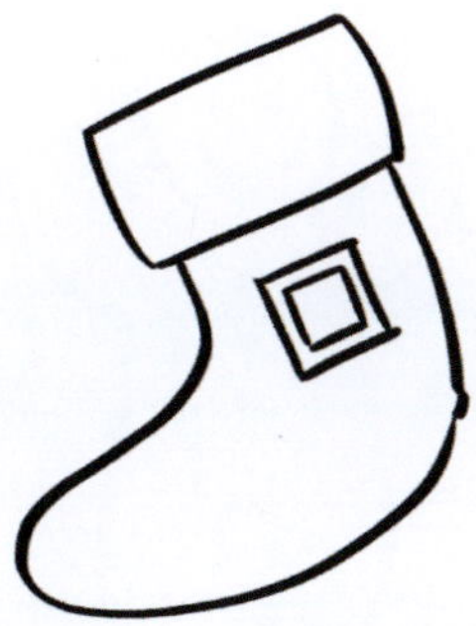

5

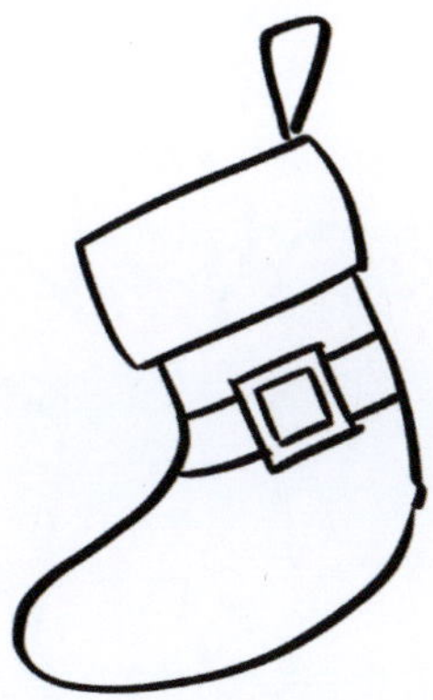

6

DAY 60

Gingerbread man

DAY 61

Angel

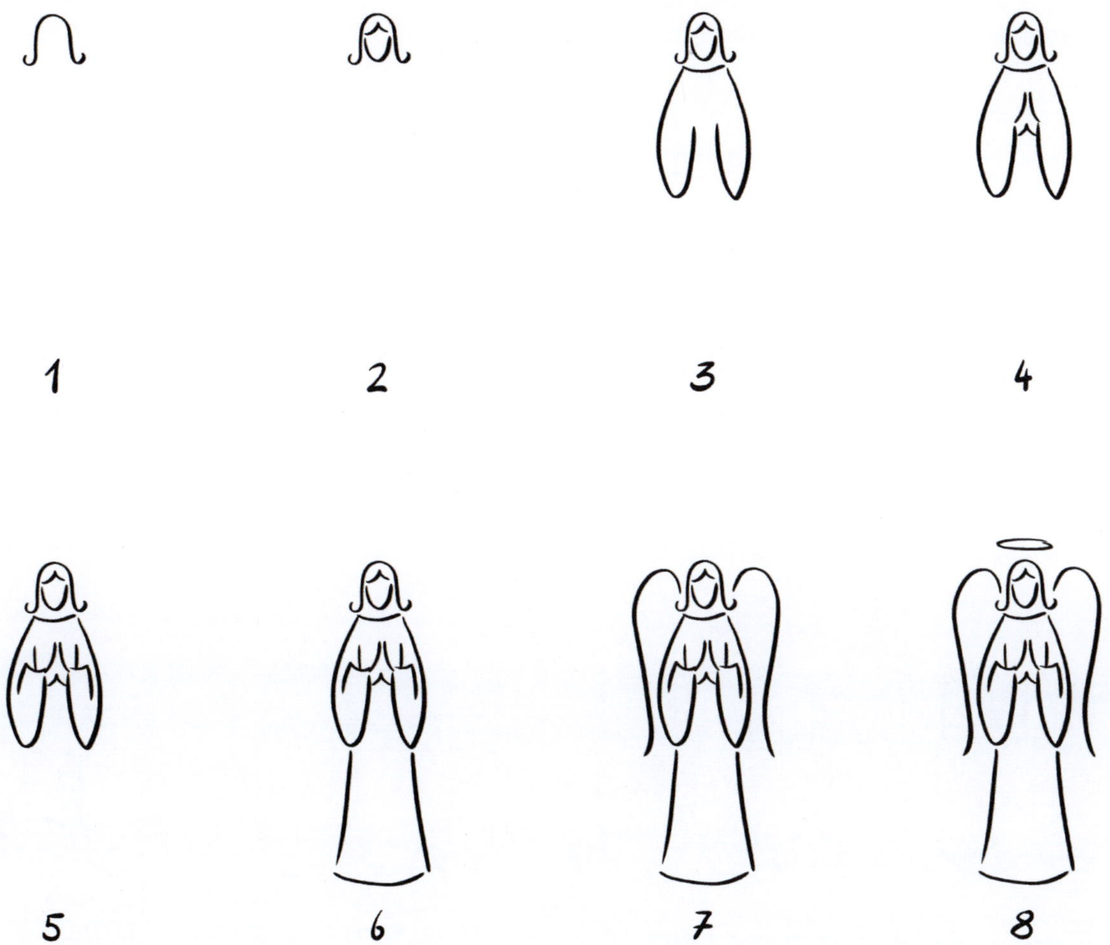

Toy train

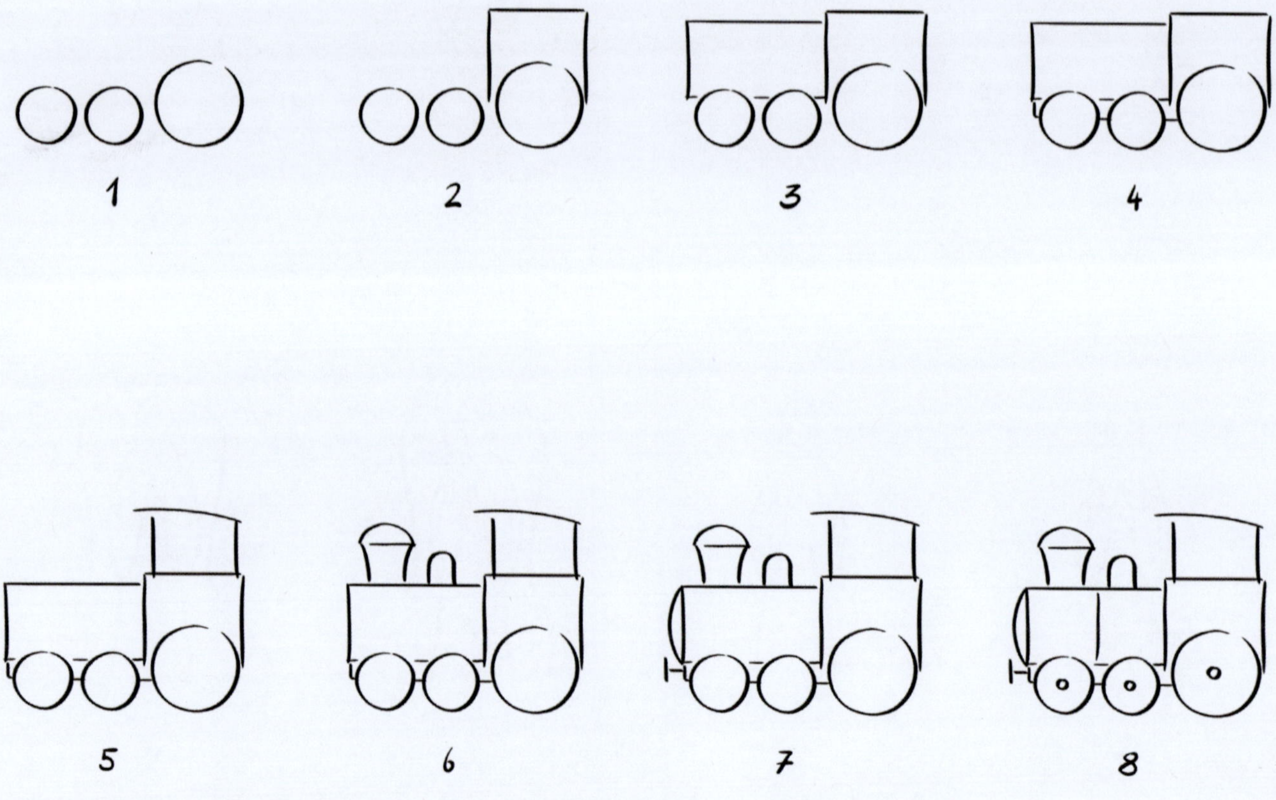

DAY 63

Goose

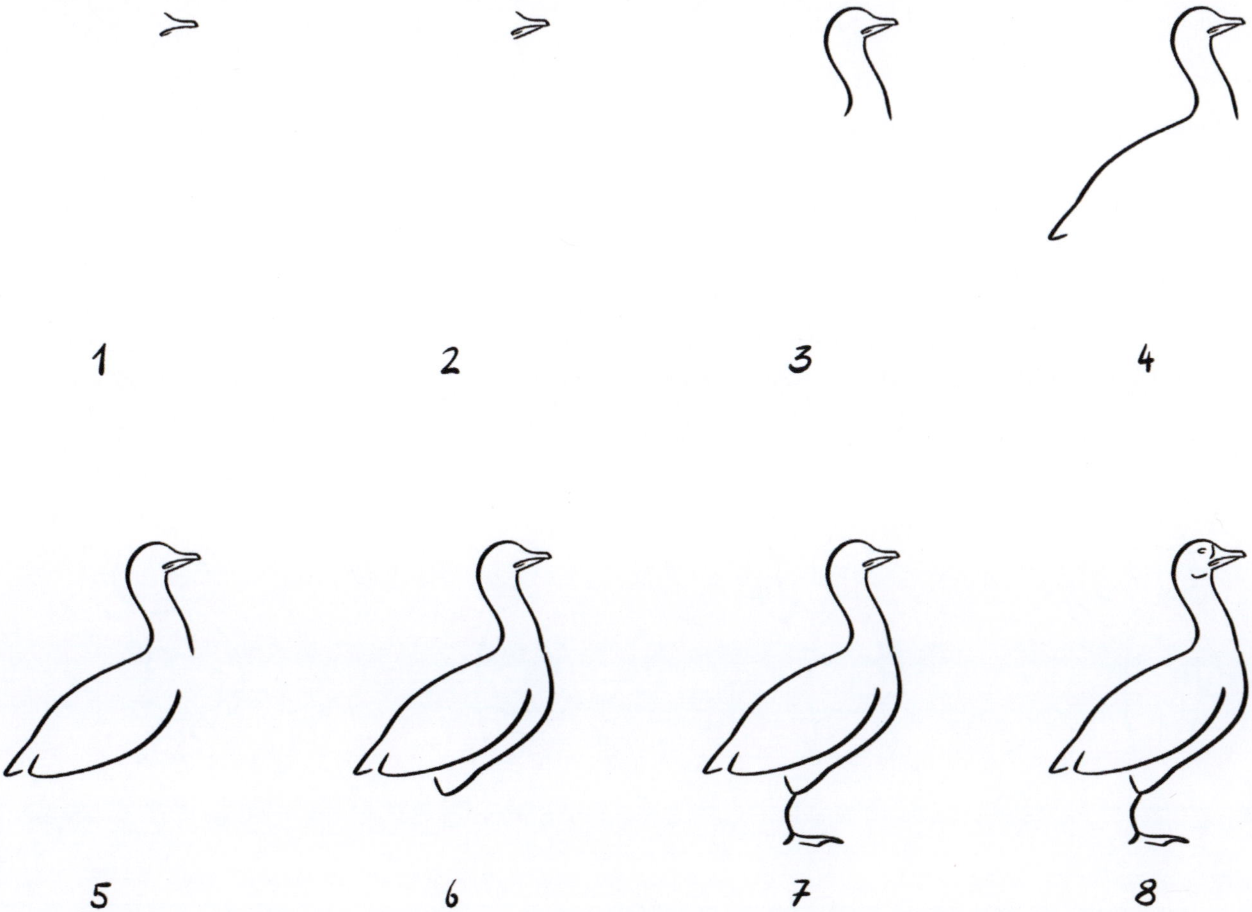

DAY 64

Robot

DAY 65

Rocket

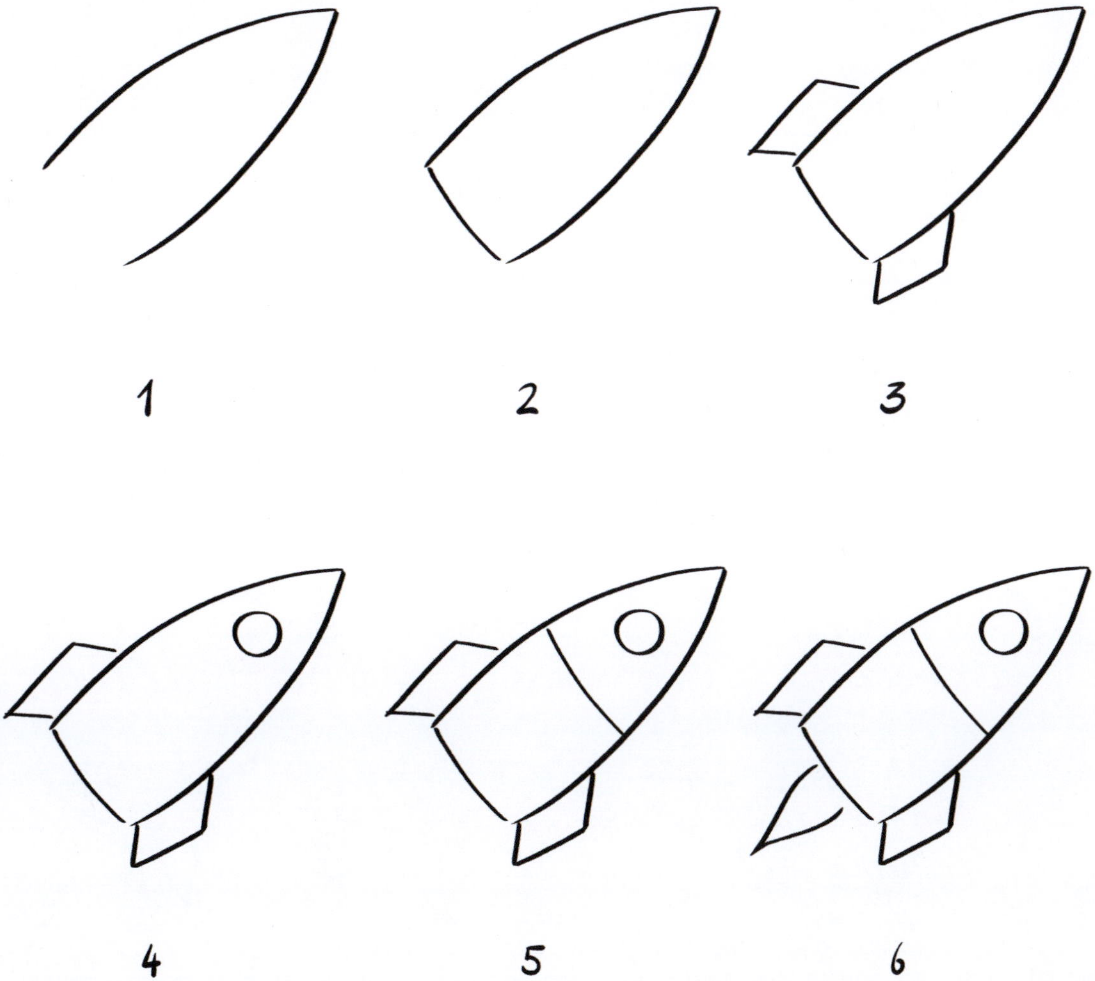

DAY 66

Shark

DAY 67

Venus flytrap

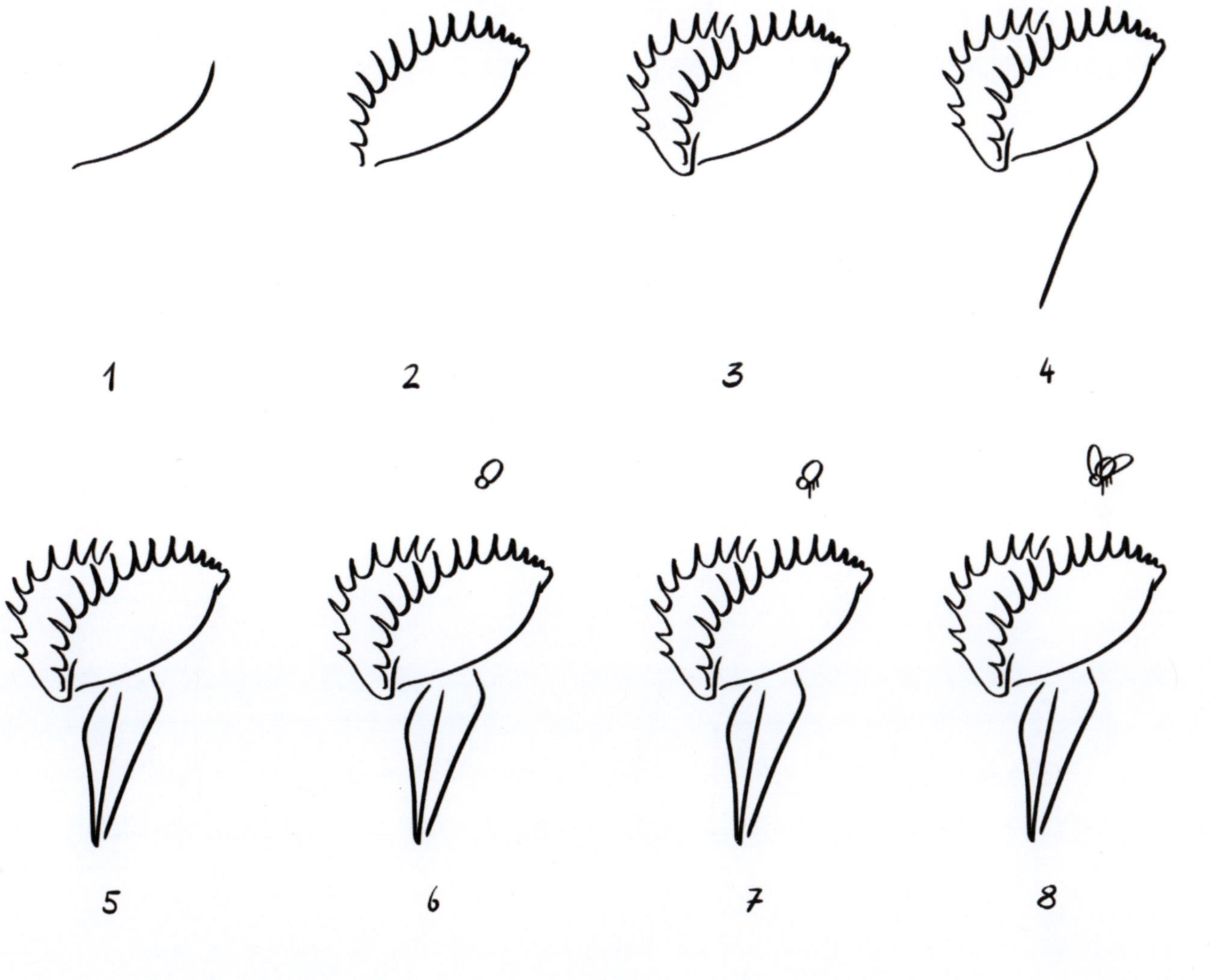

DAY 68

Saw

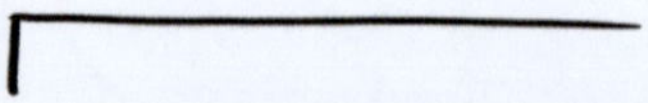

1

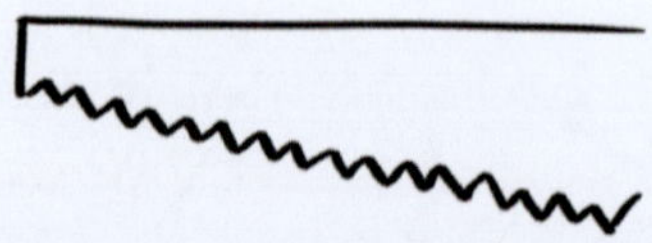

2

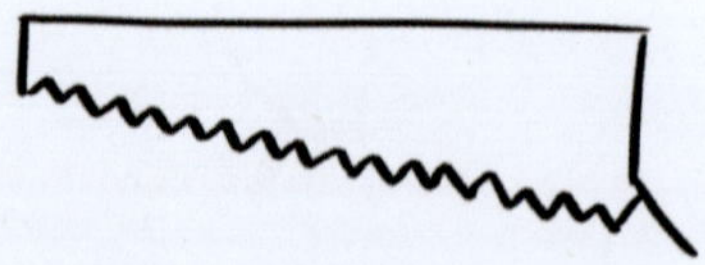

3

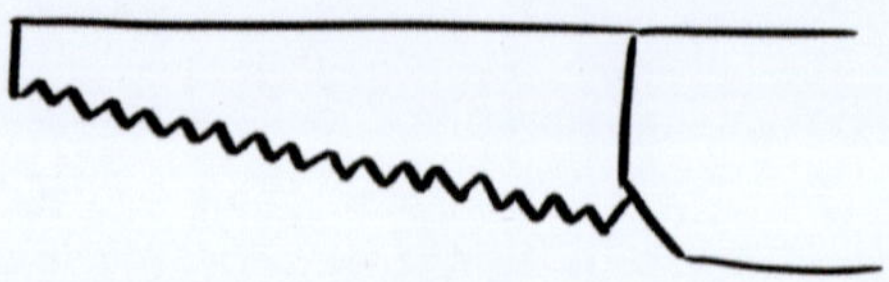

4

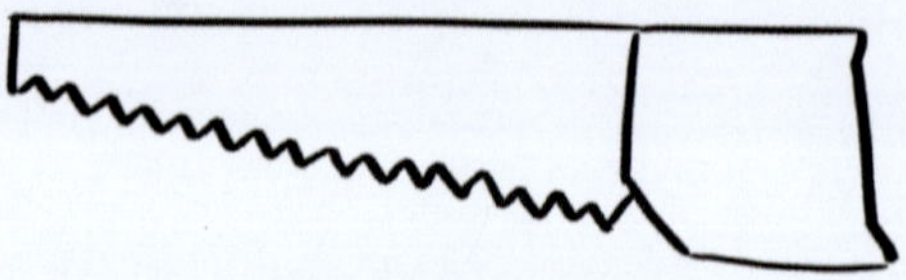

5

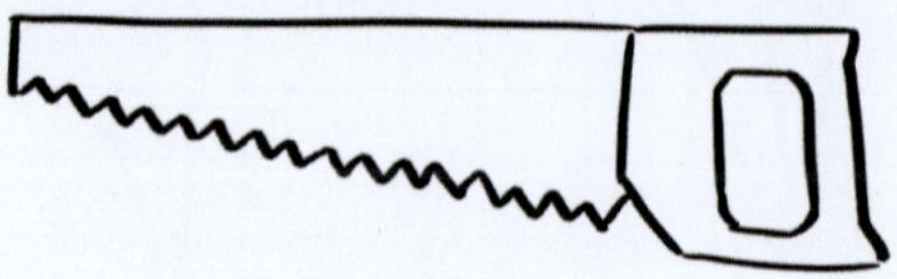

6

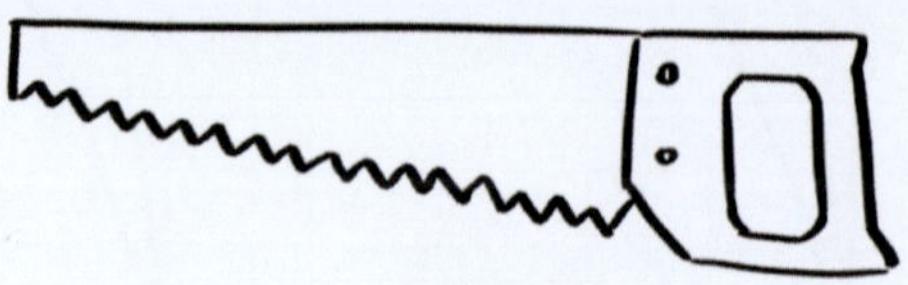

7

DAY 69

Scroll

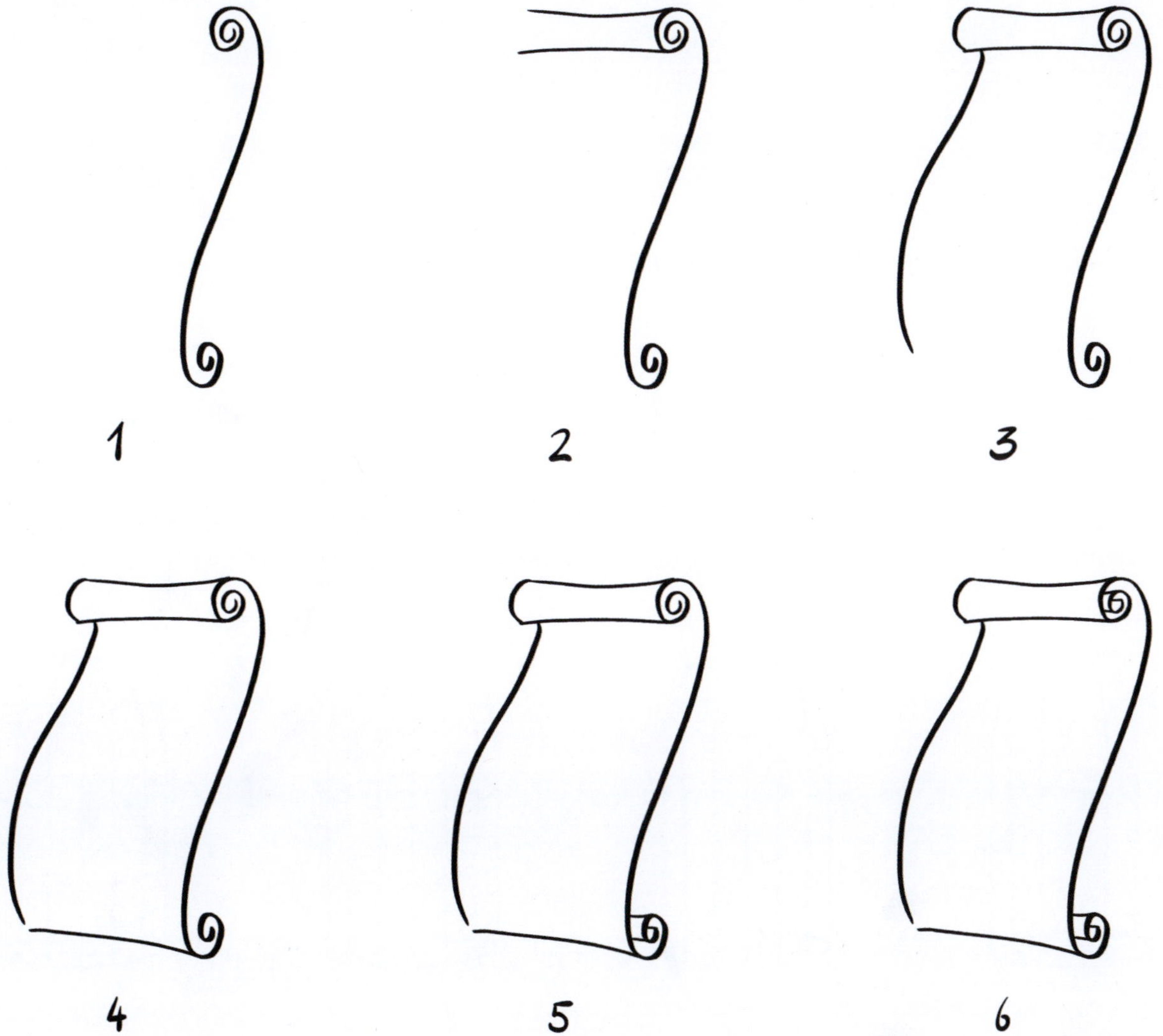

DAY 70

Birdcage

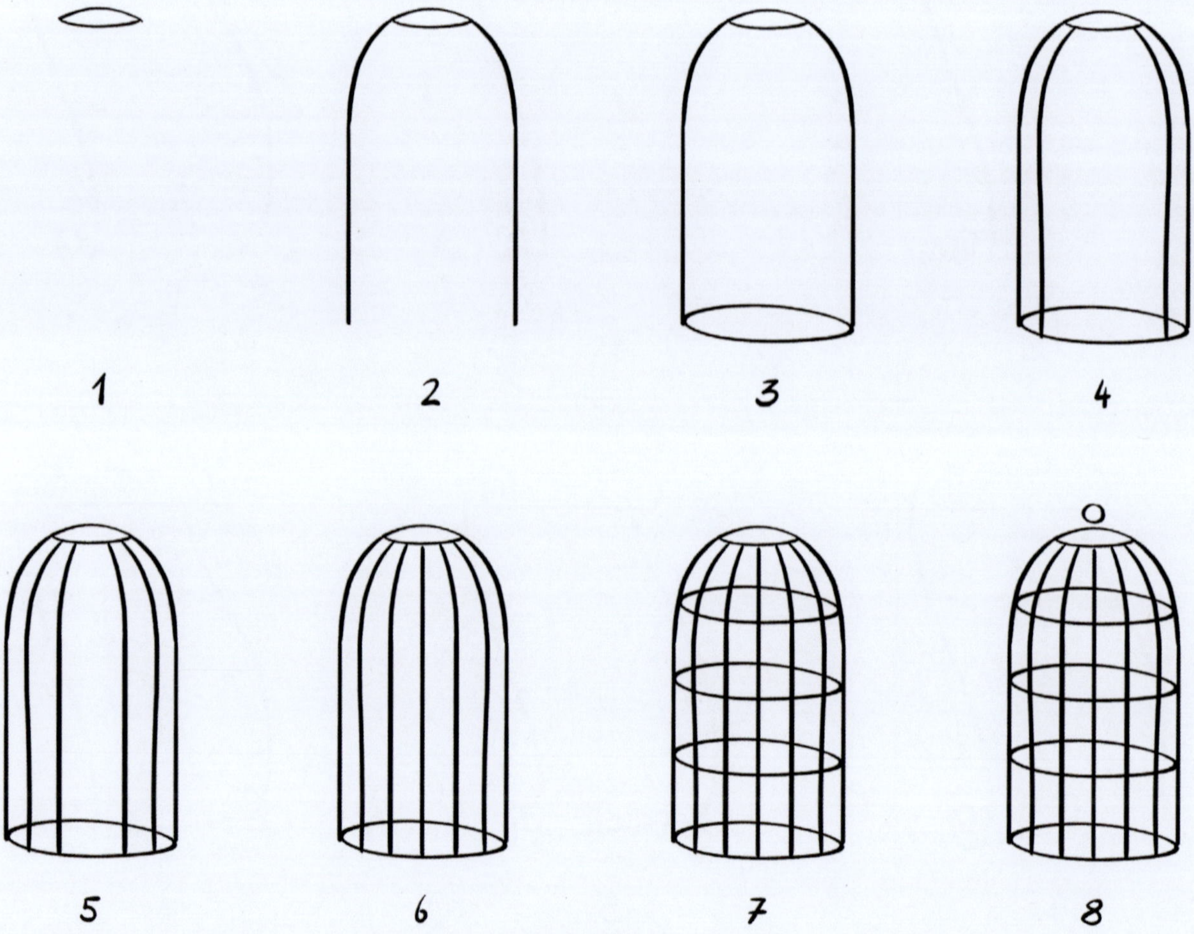

Sneaking

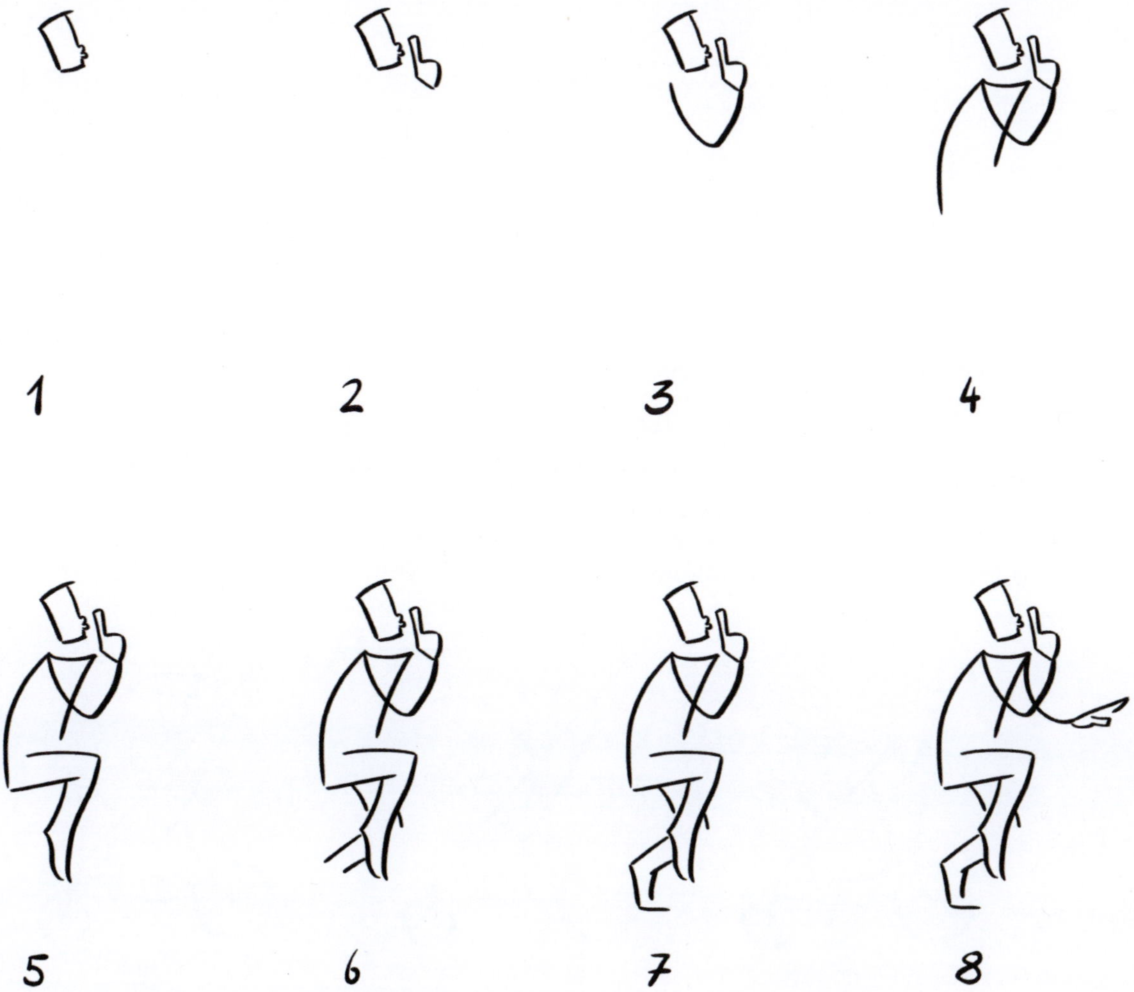

DAY 72

Buggy

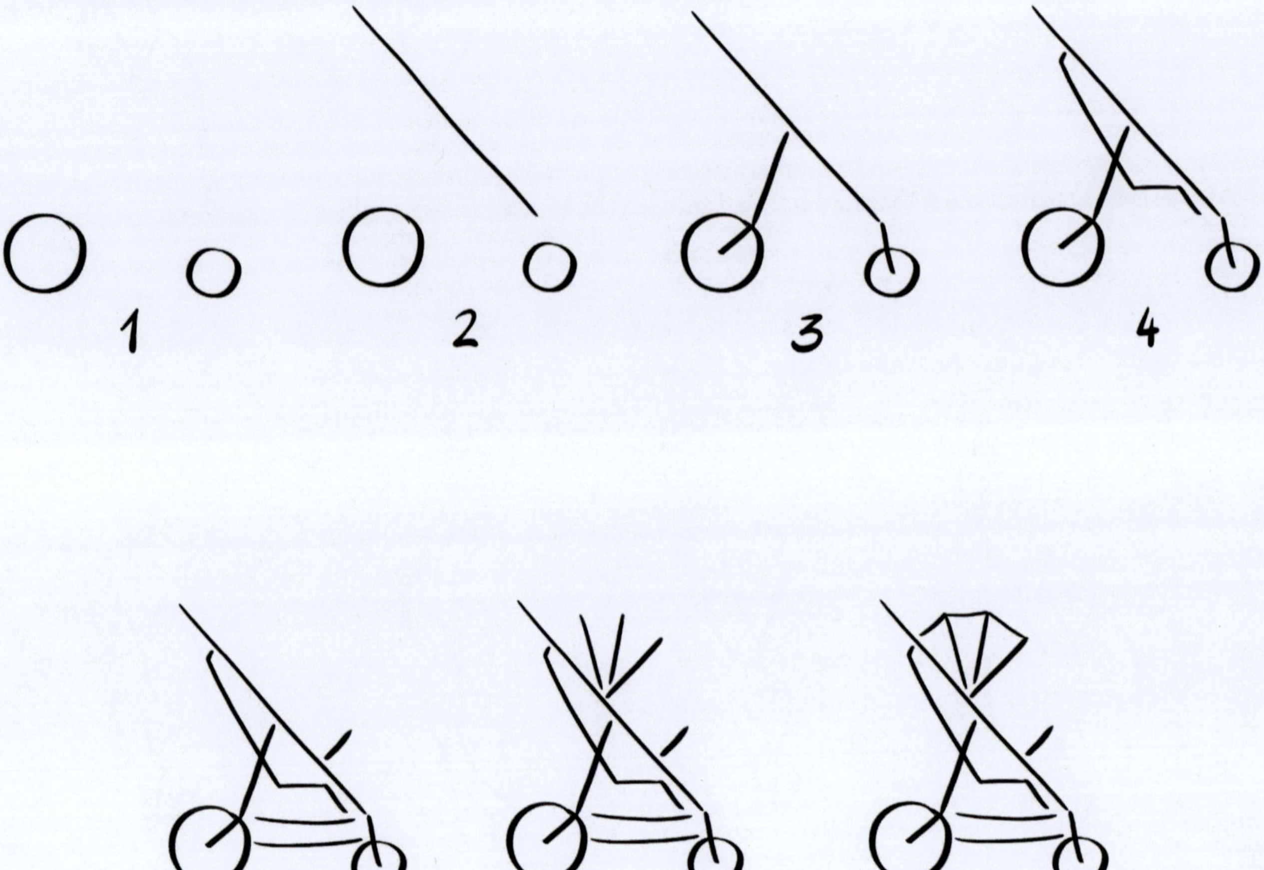

DAY 73

Mushroom

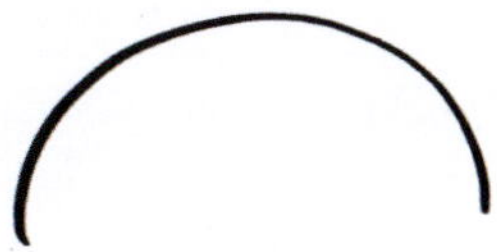

1

2

3

4

5

6

DAY 74

Balancing

DAY 75

Scuba diver

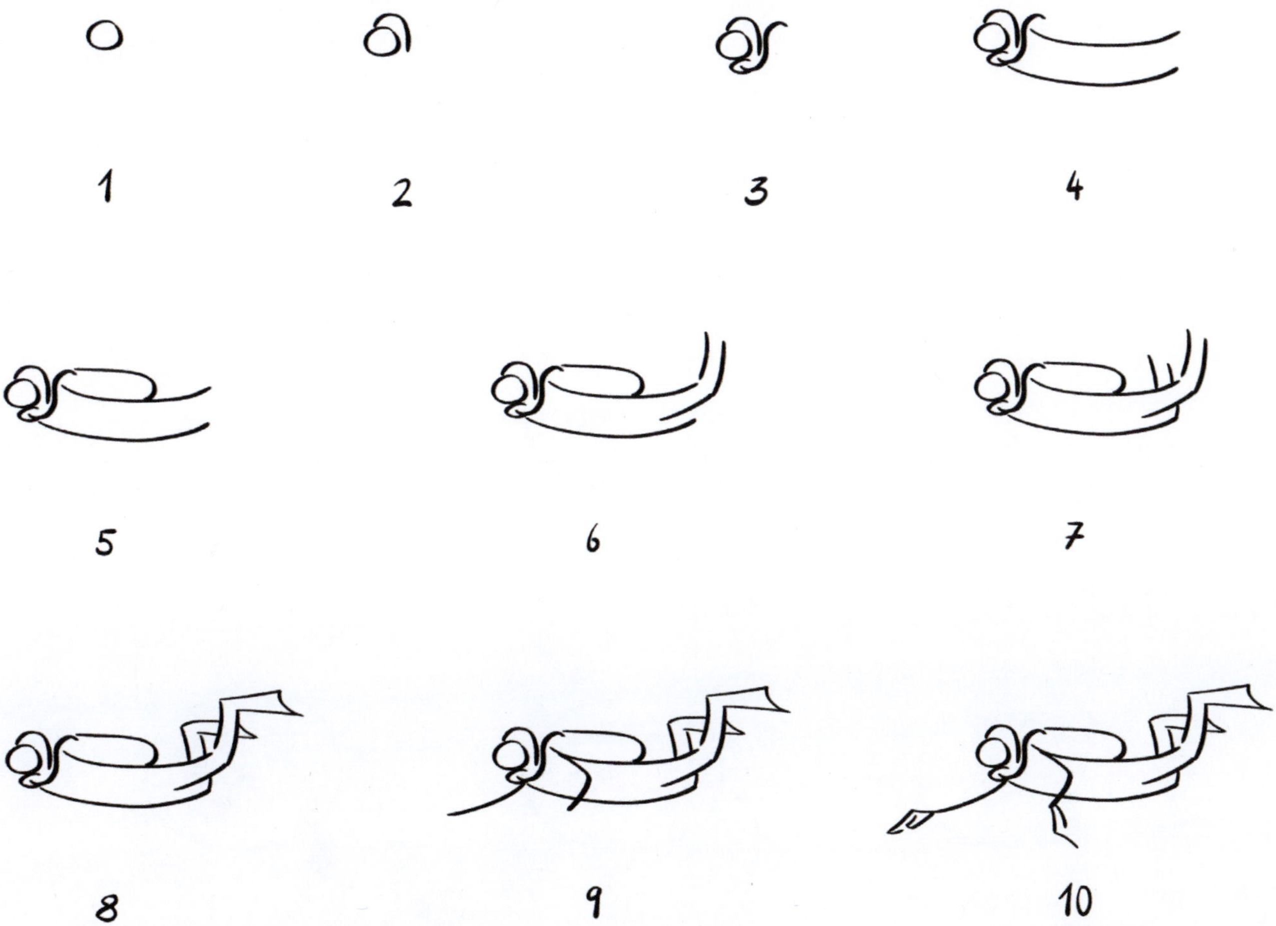

DAY 76

Fishbowl

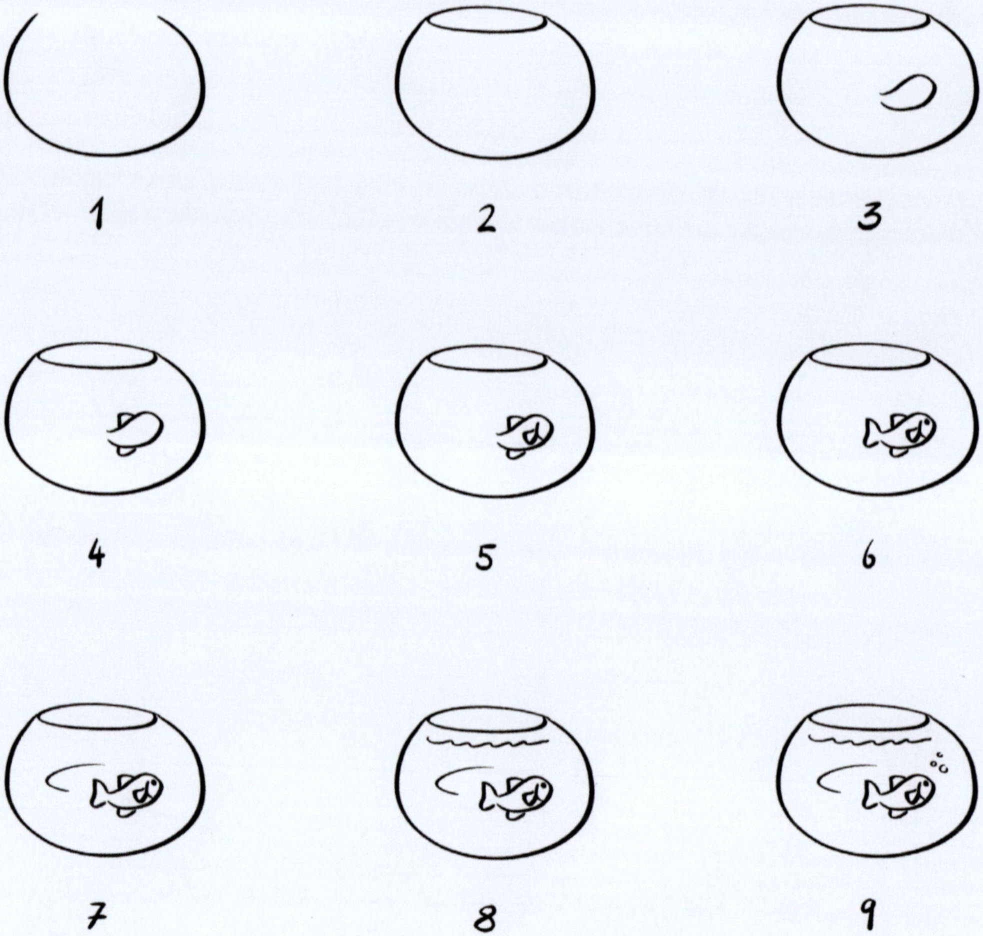

DAY 77

Beer

1

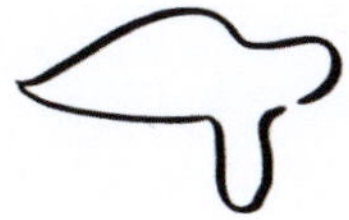

2

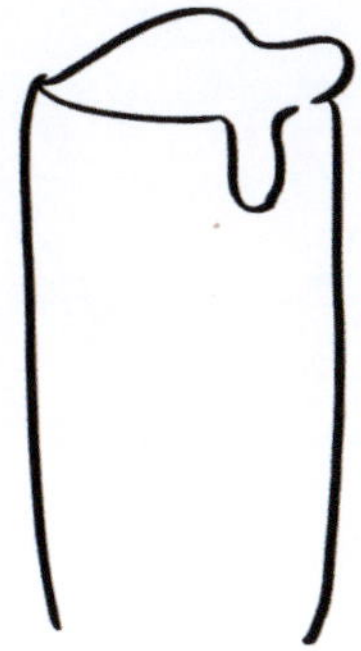

3

4

5

6

DAY 78

Broom

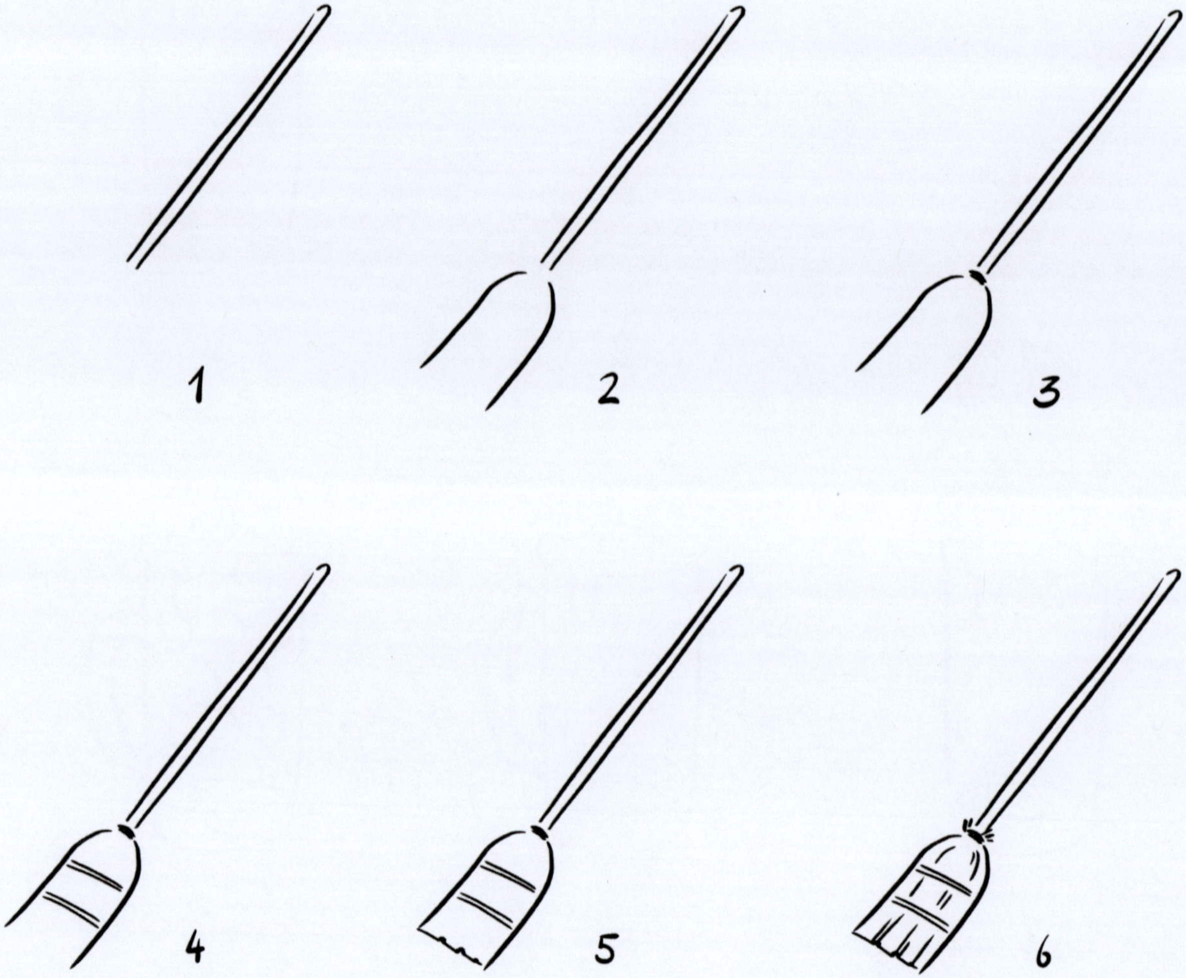

DAY 79

Clown

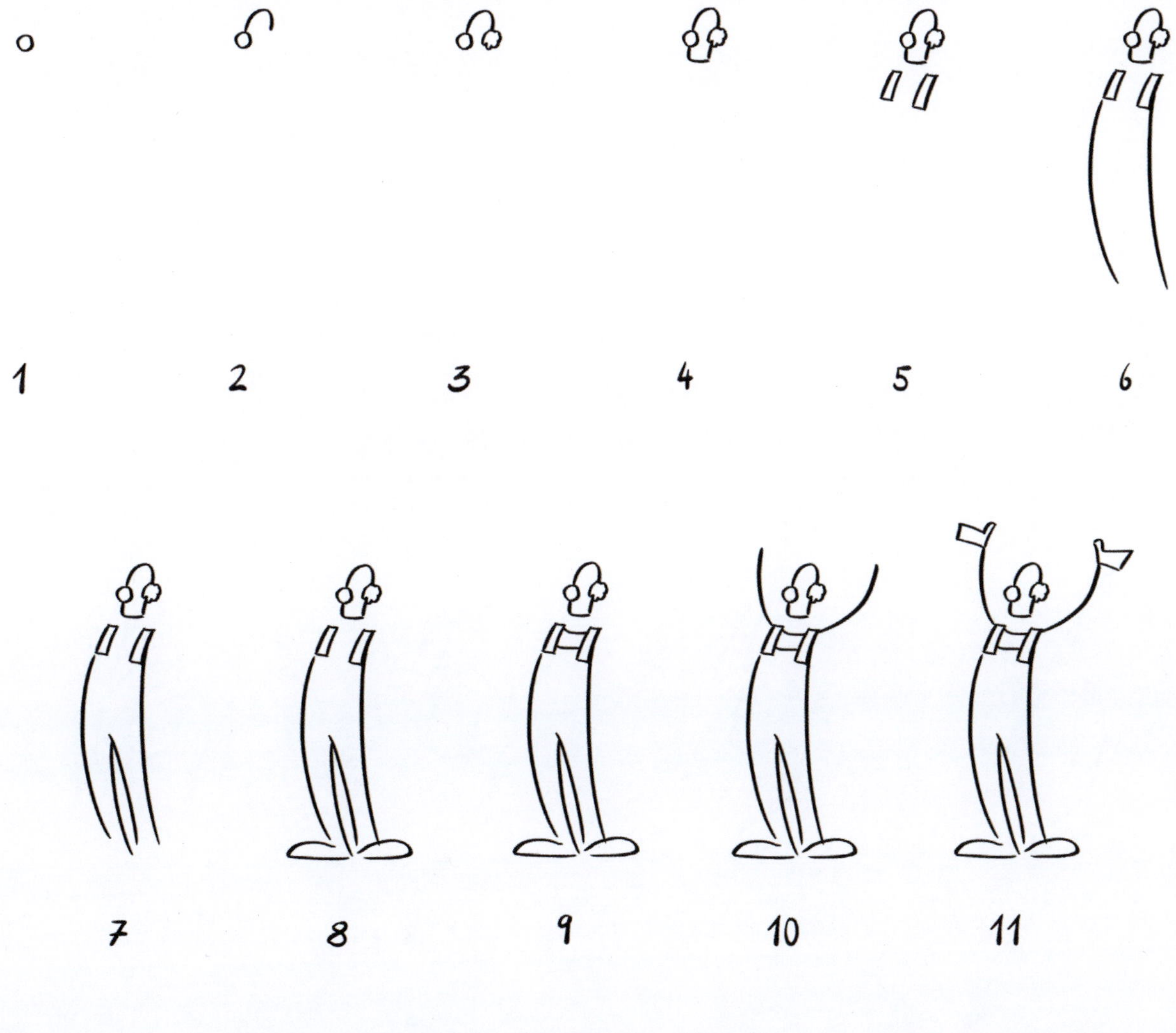

DAY 80

Perfect

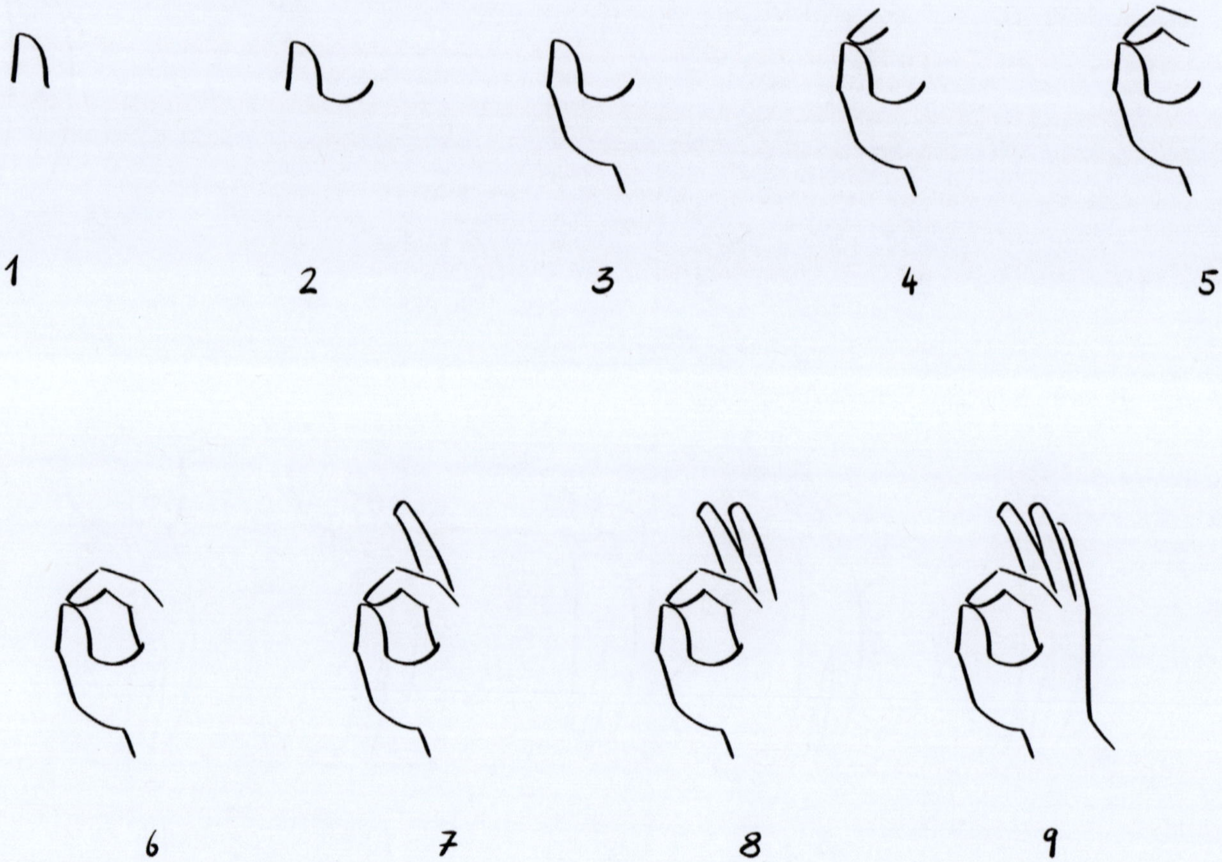

DAY 81

Pliers

1

2

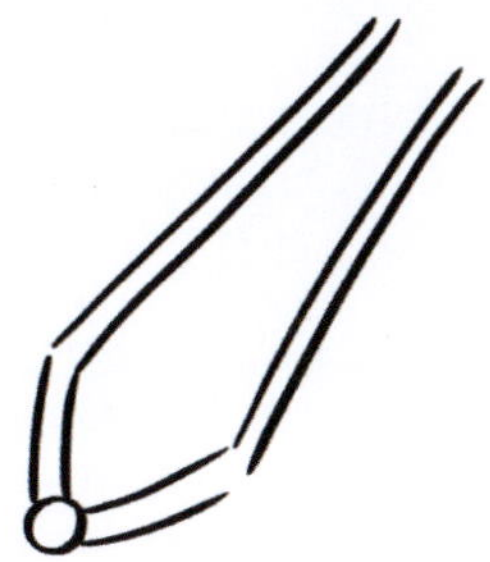

3

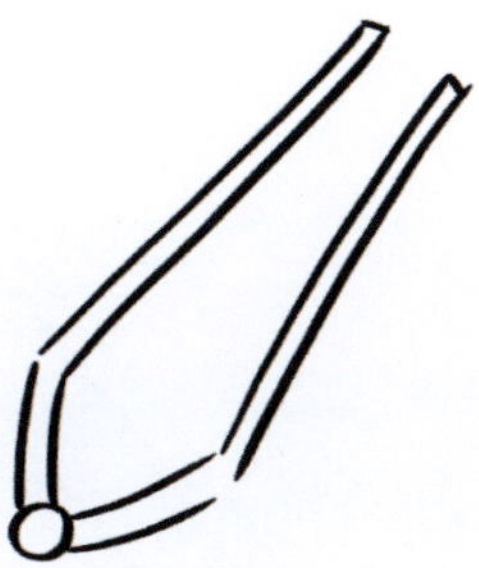

4

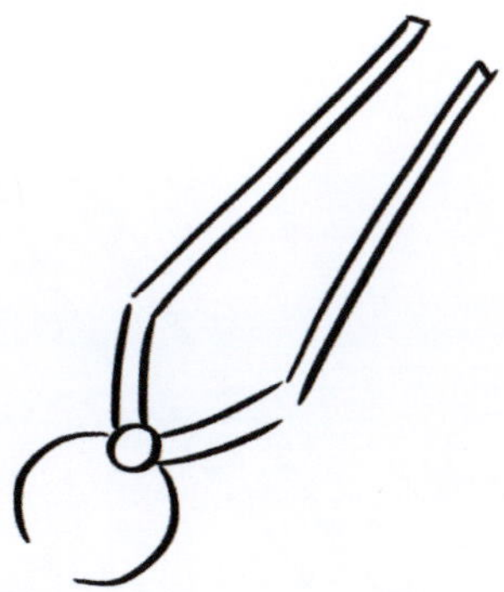

5

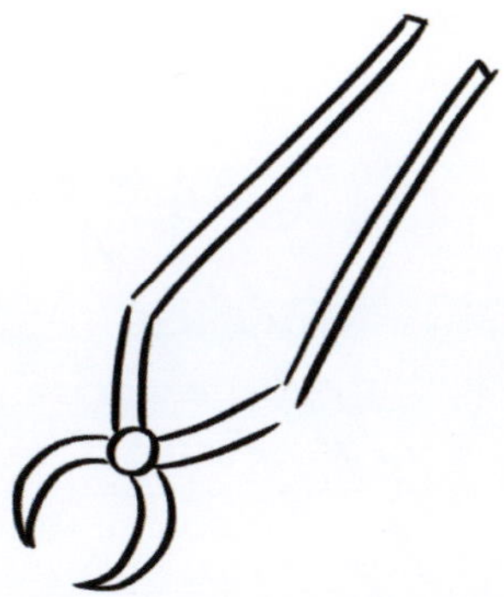

6

DAY 82

Feather

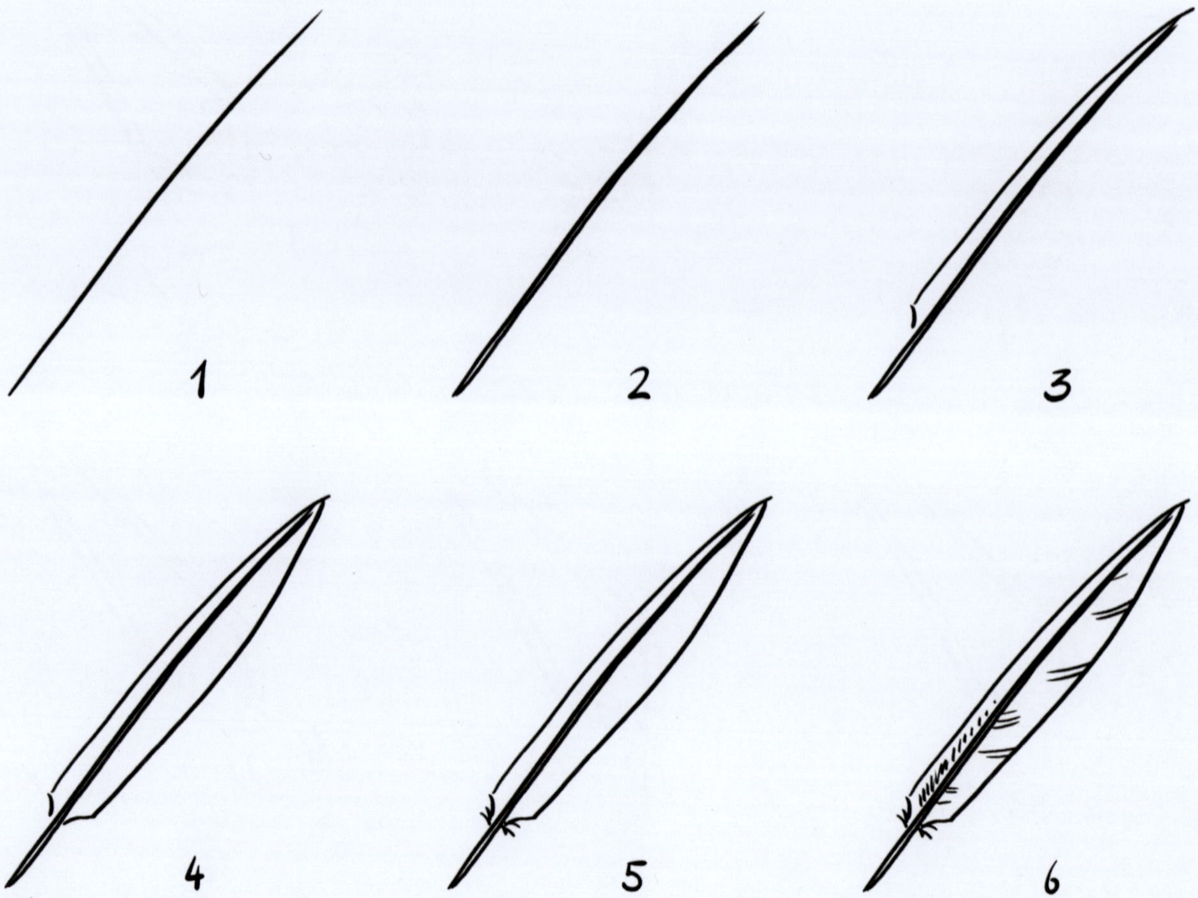

DAY 83

Eel

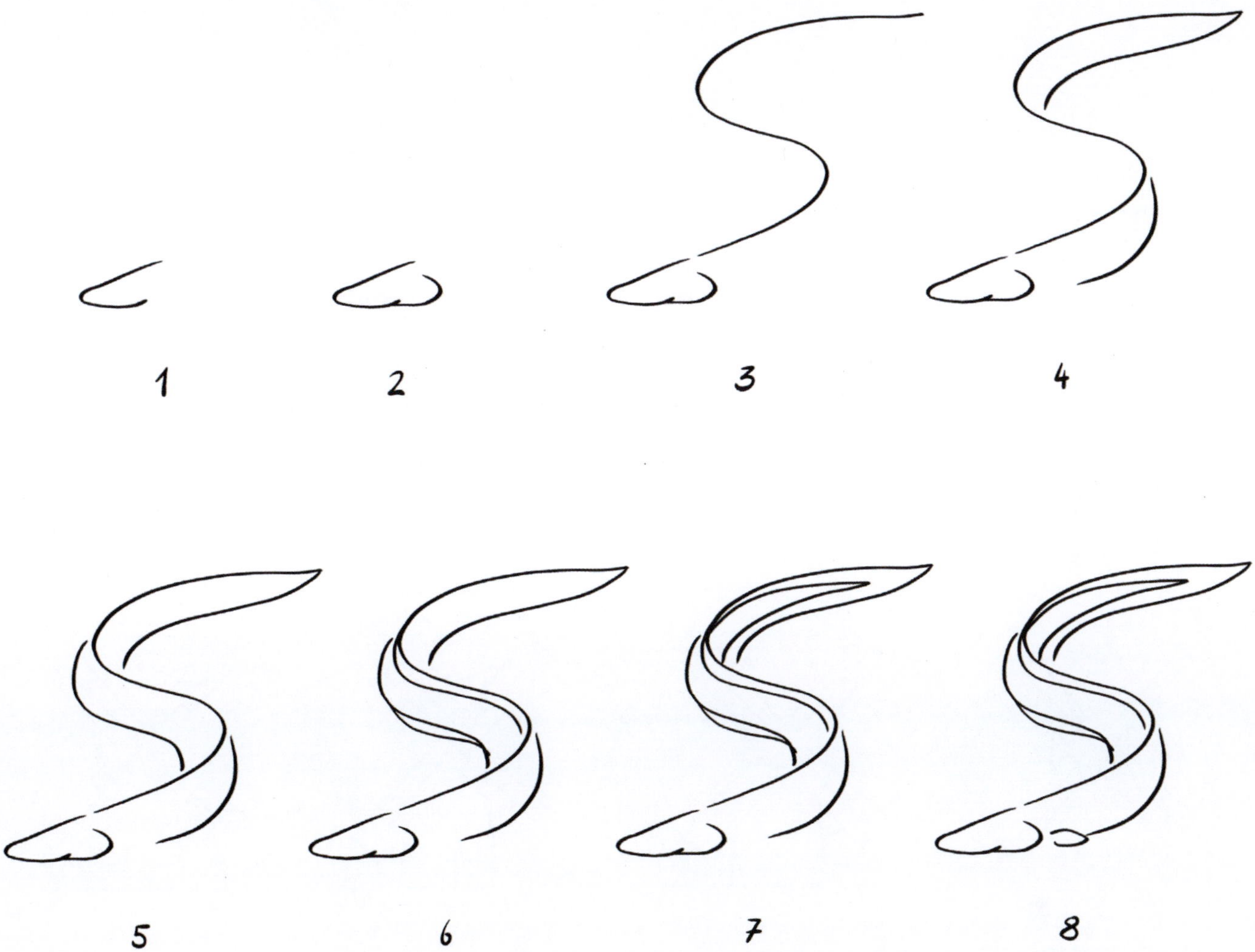

DAY 84

Windmill

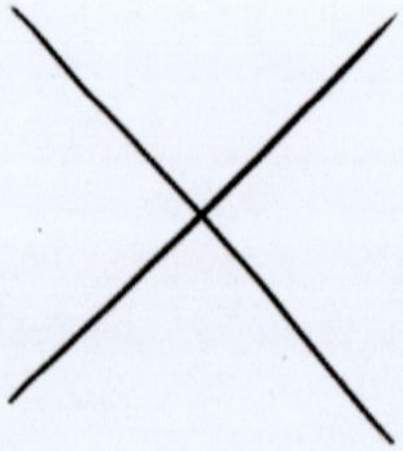

1

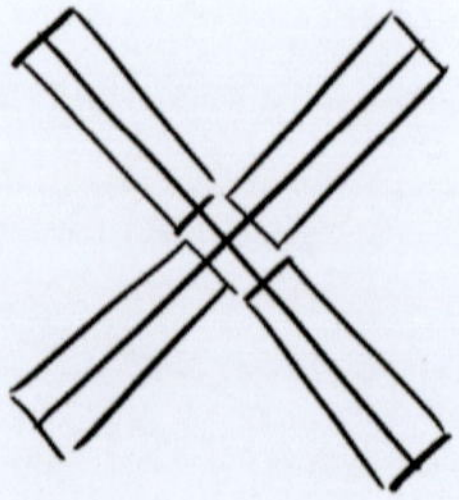

2

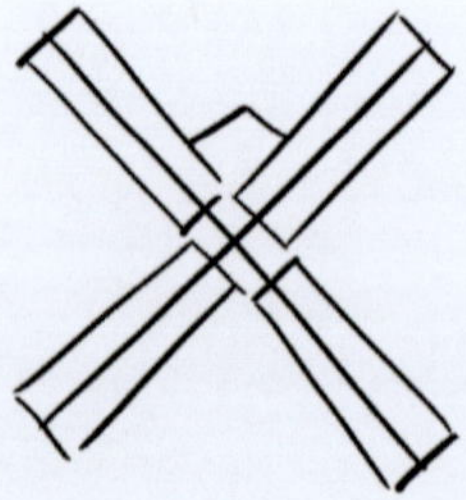

3

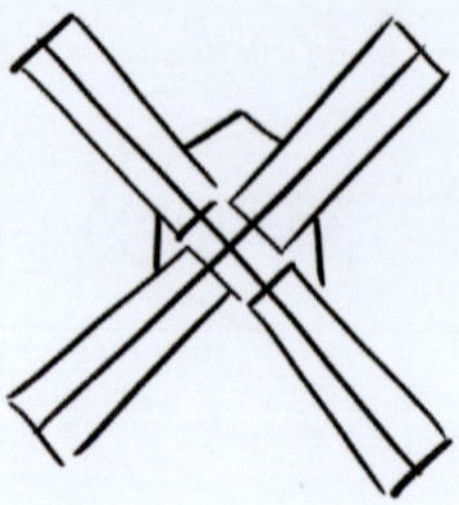

4

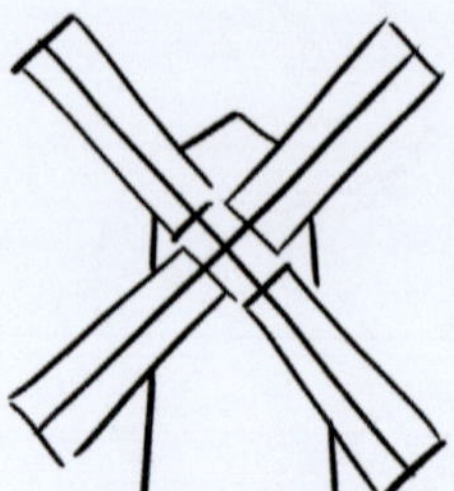

5

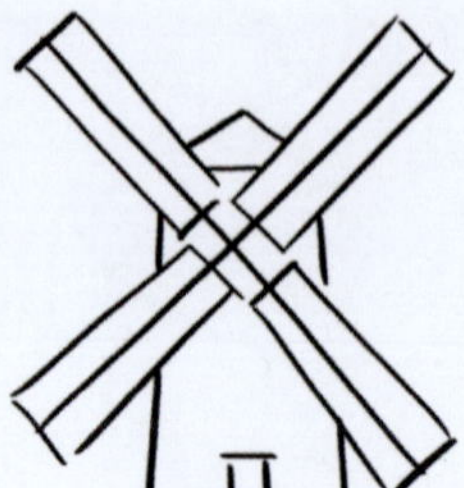

6

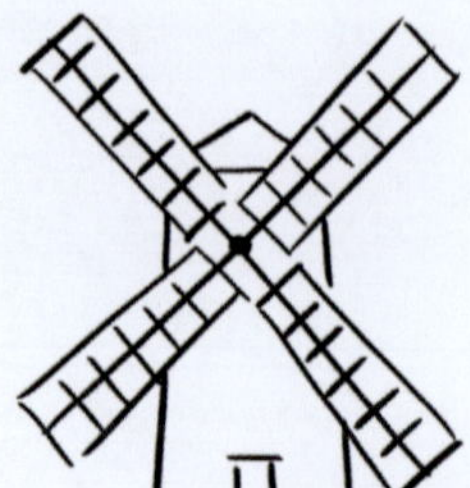

7

DAY 85

Inkwell

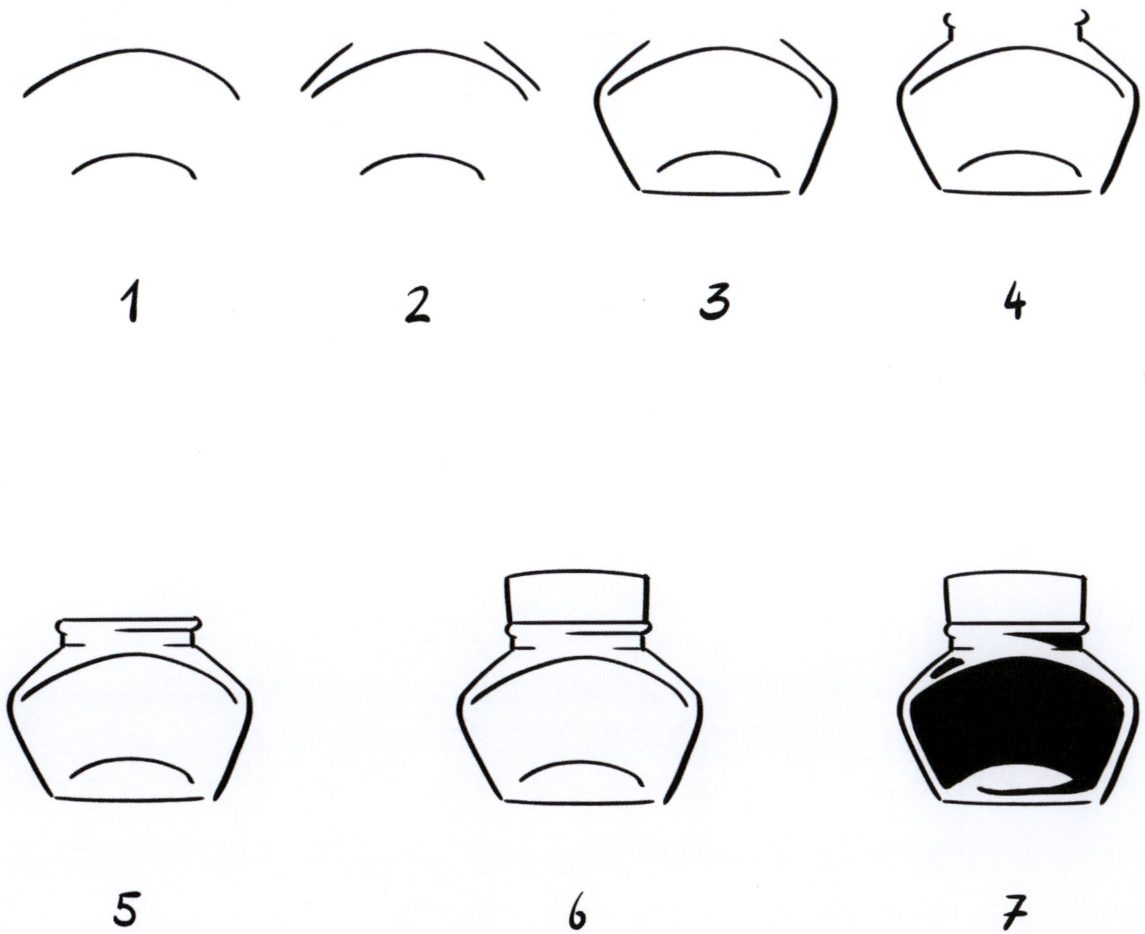

DAY 86

Razorblade

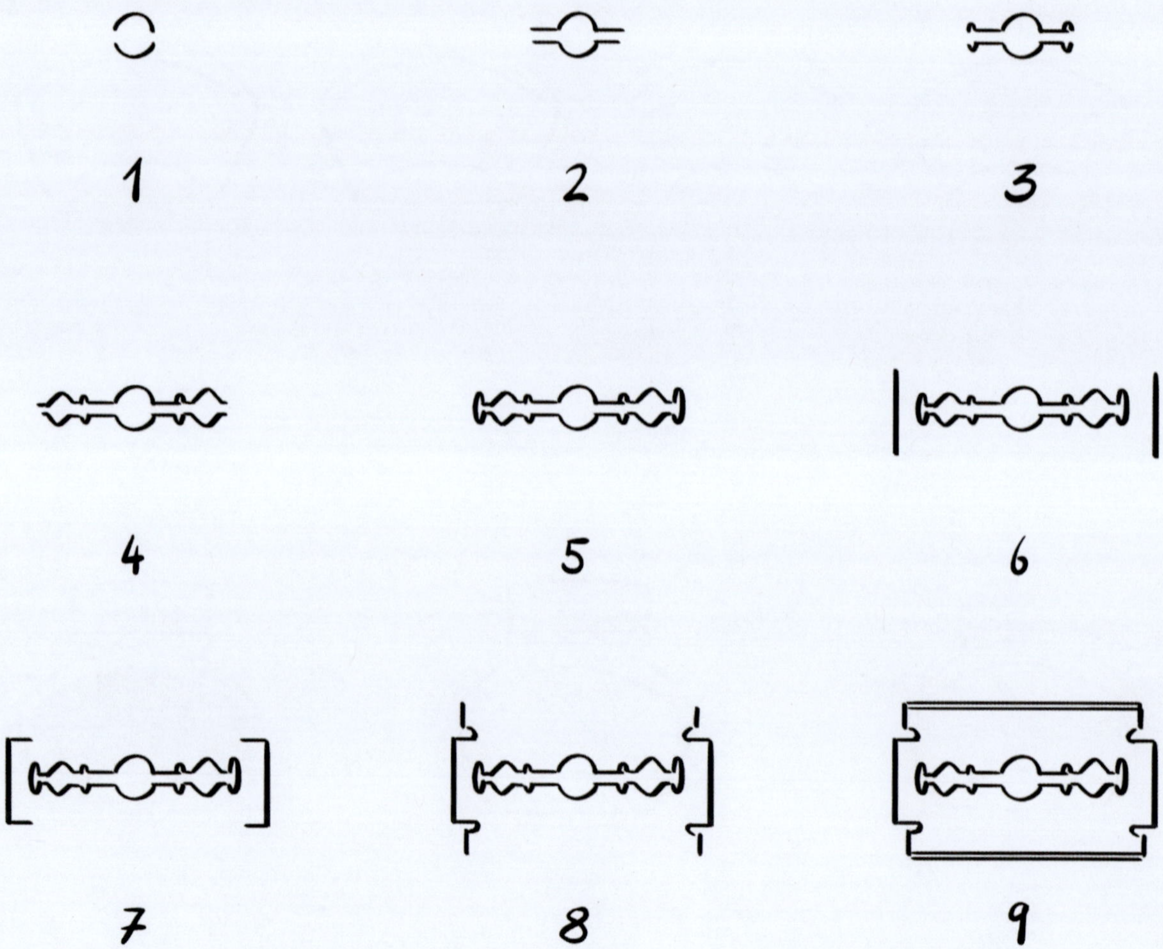

DAY 87

Soap

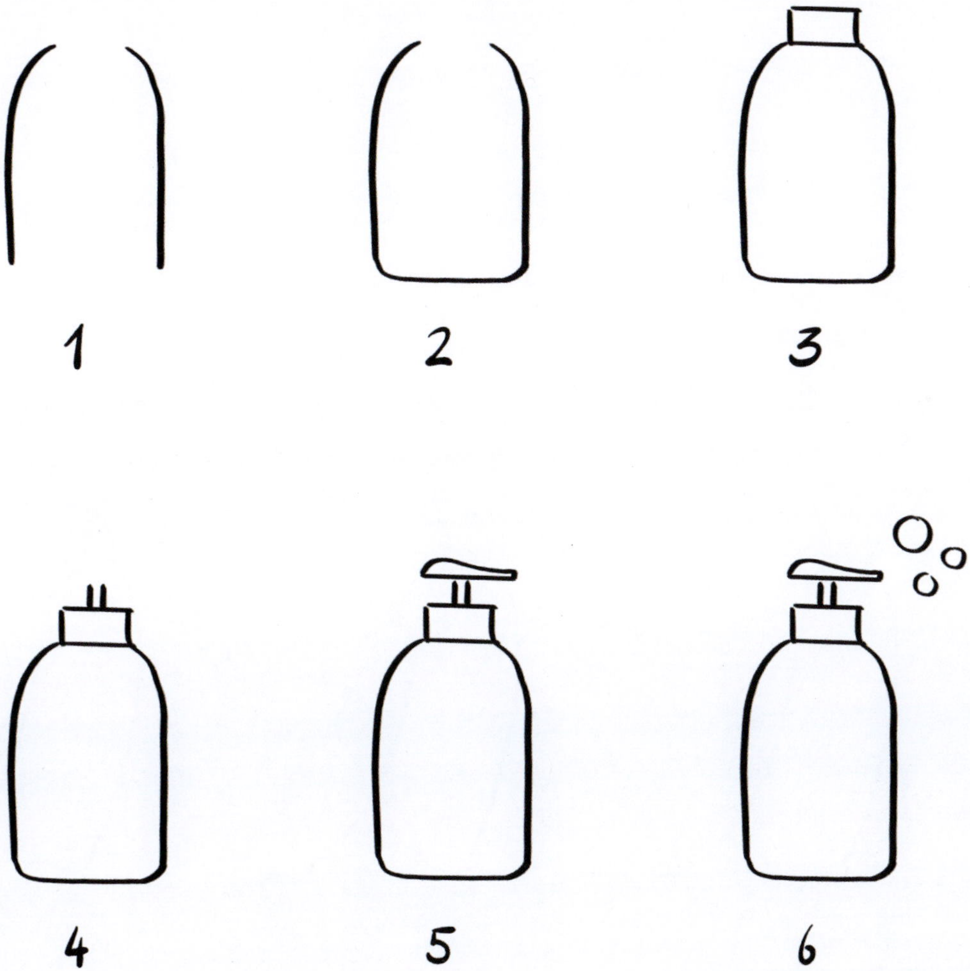

DAY 88

Ghost

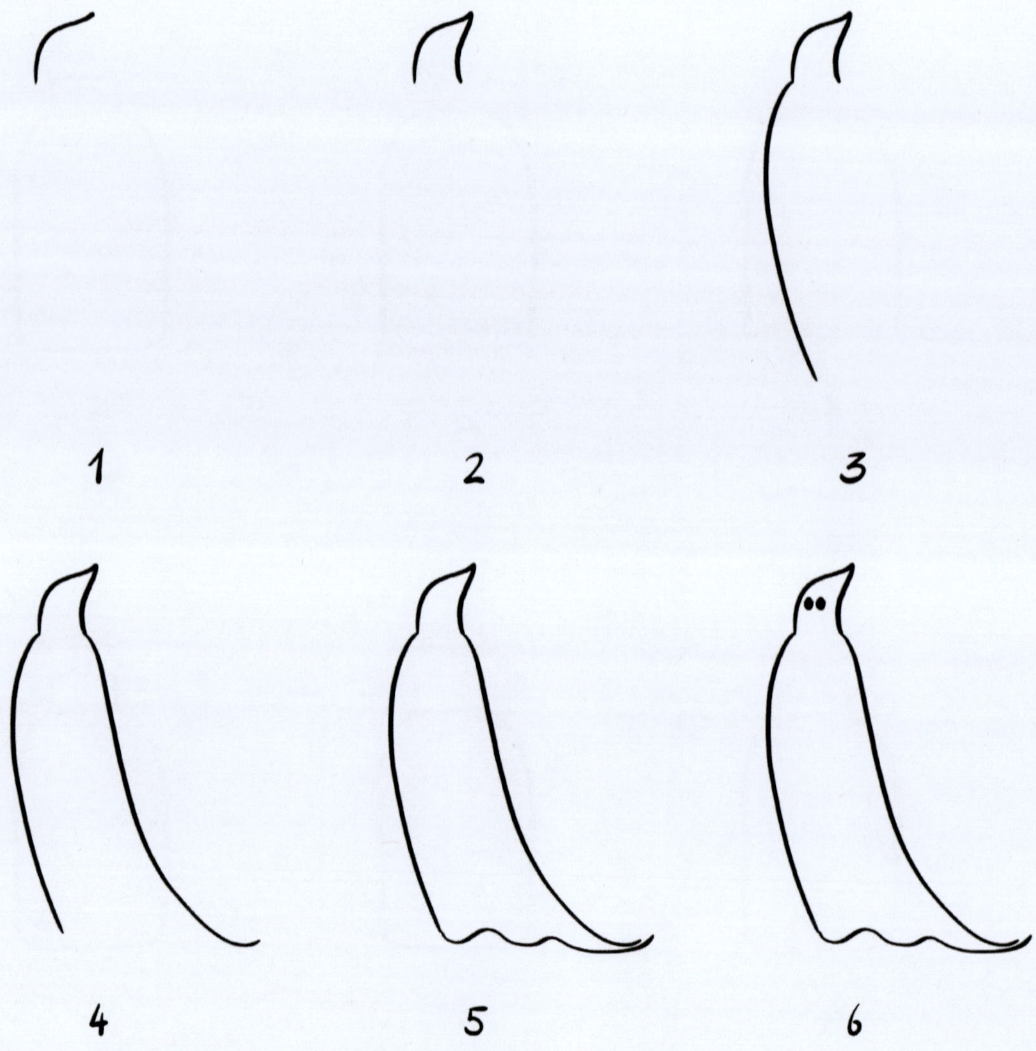

DAY 89

Nose

1

2

3

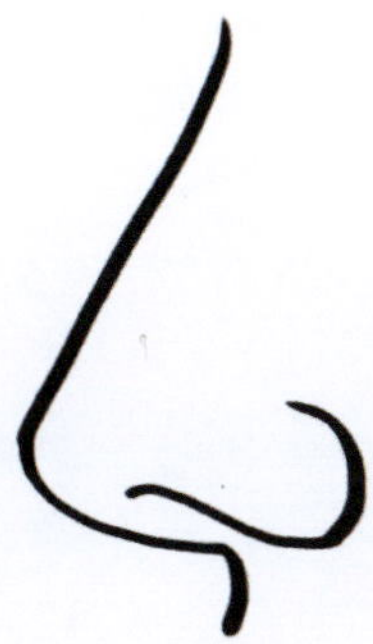

4

5

DAY 90

Sleep

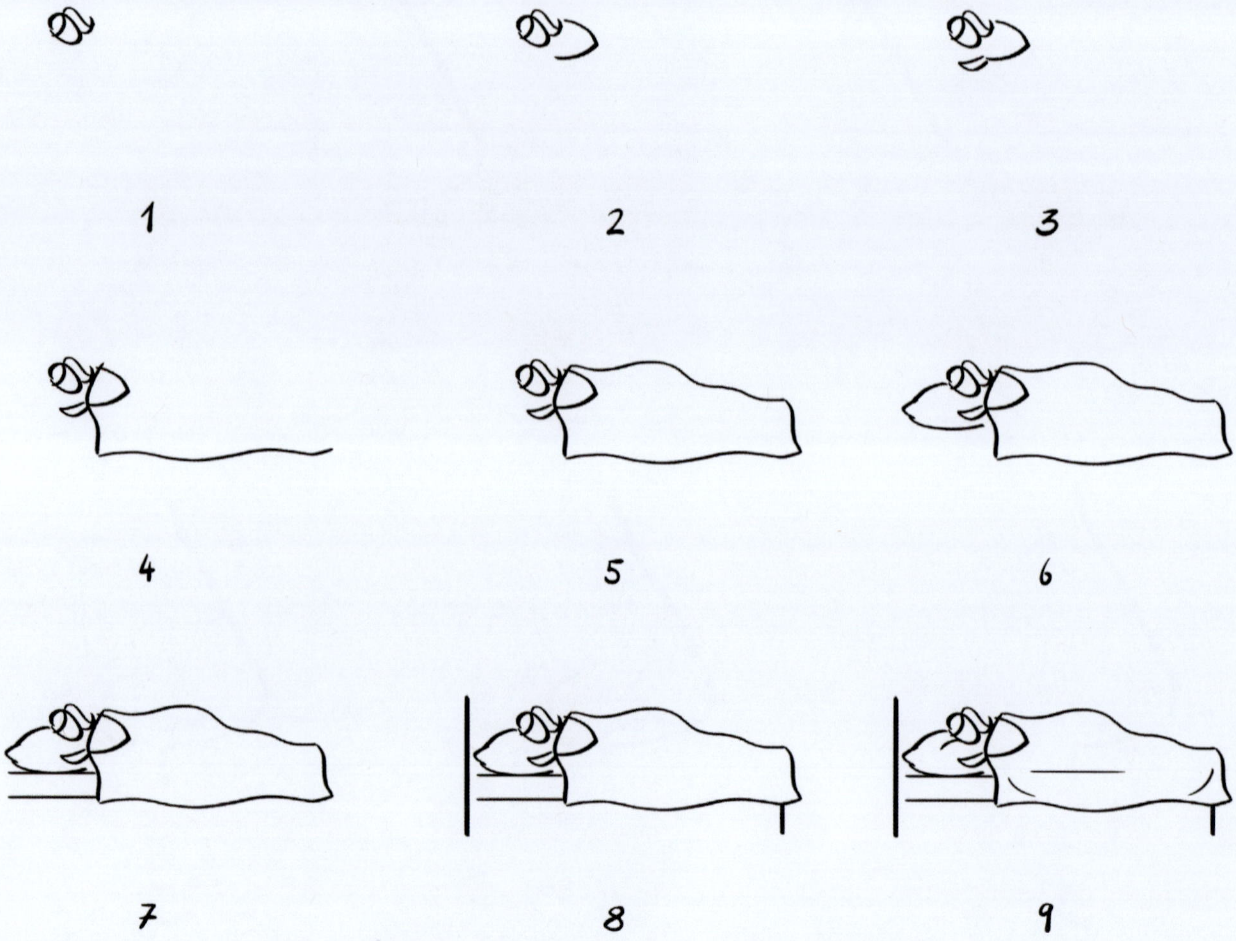

DAY 91

Trashcan

DAY 92

Pizza slice

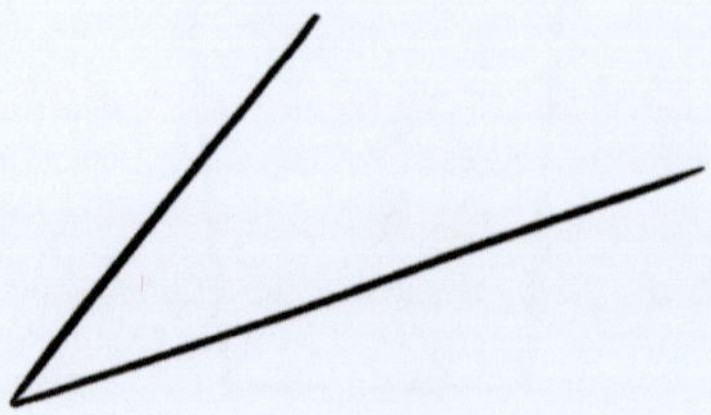

1

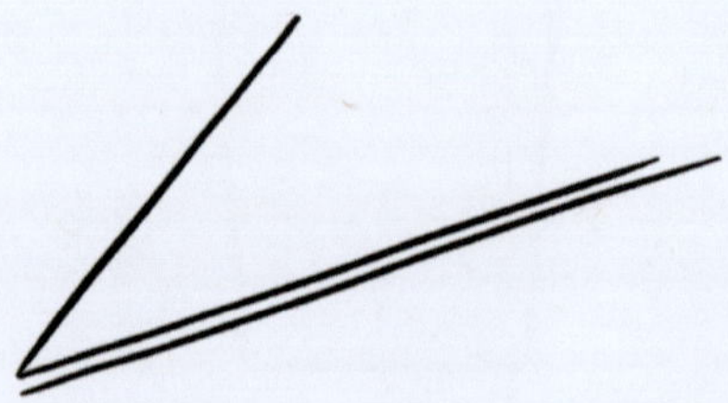

2

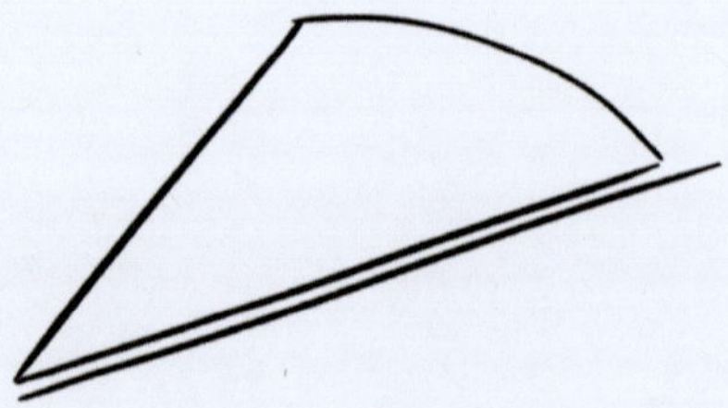

3

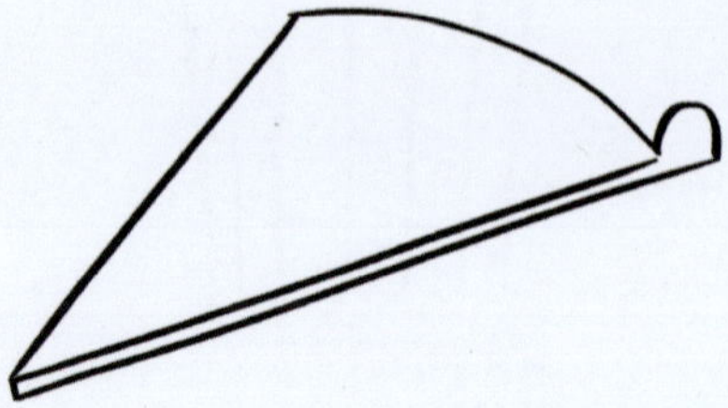

4

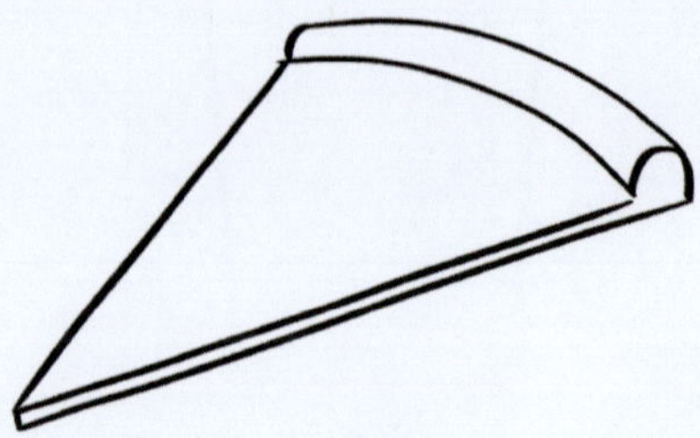

5

6

DAY 93

Serving

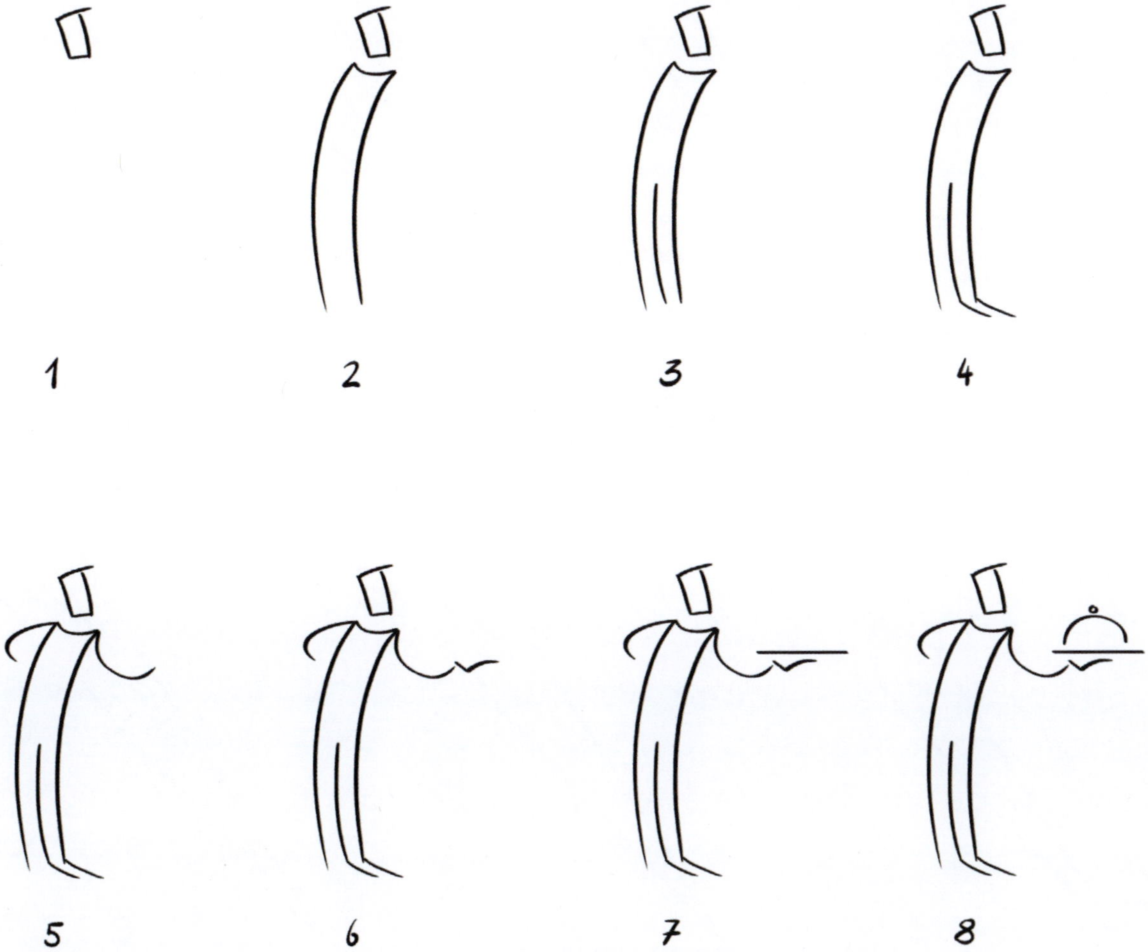

DAY 94

Carrot

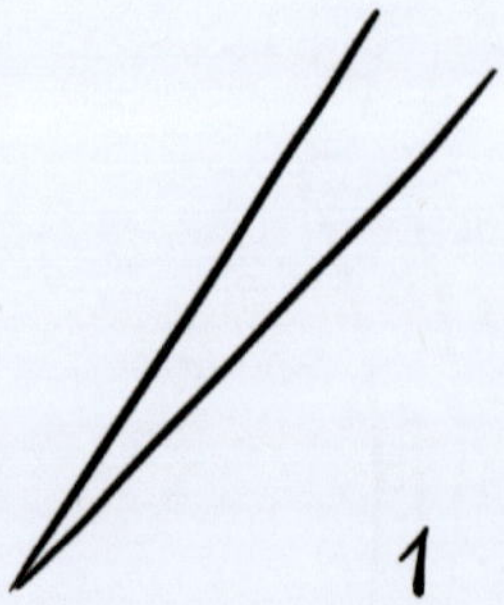

1

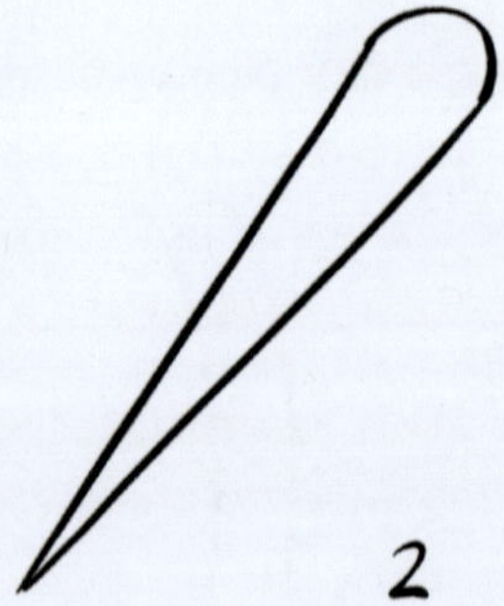

2

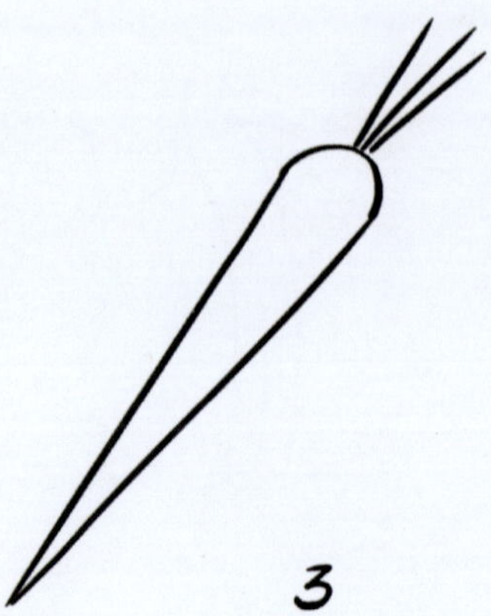

3

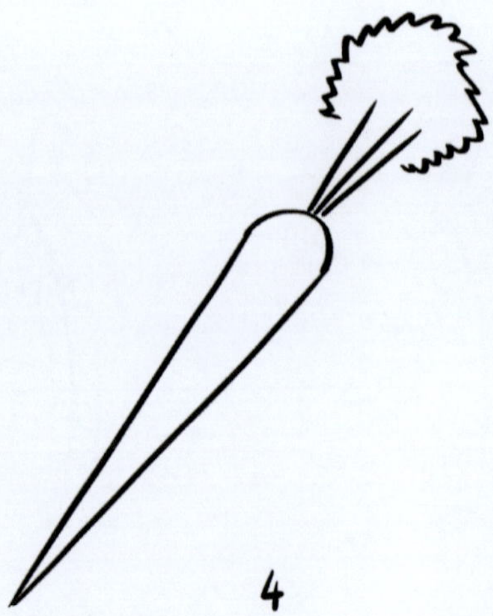

4

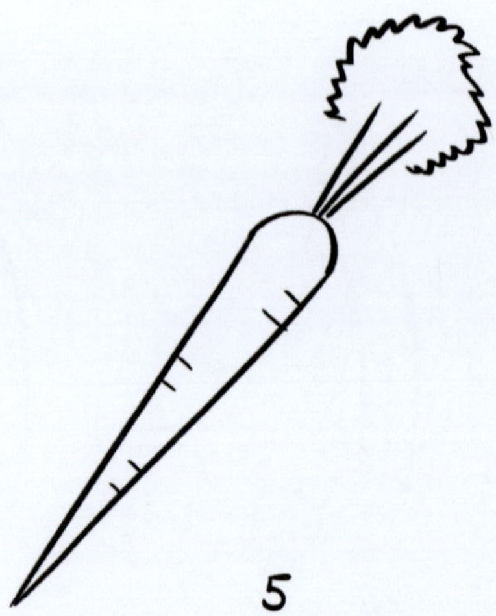

5

Letter

1

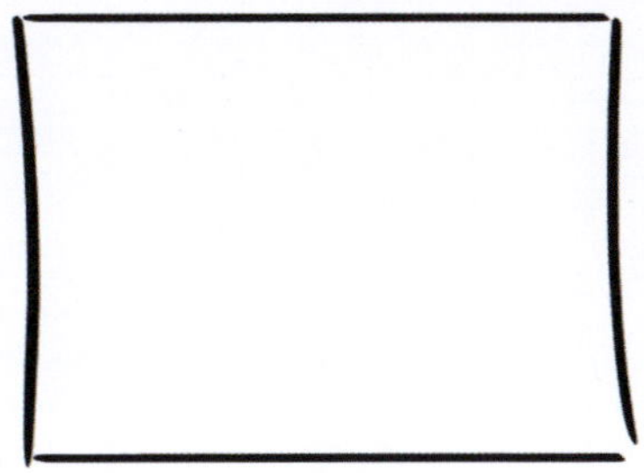

2

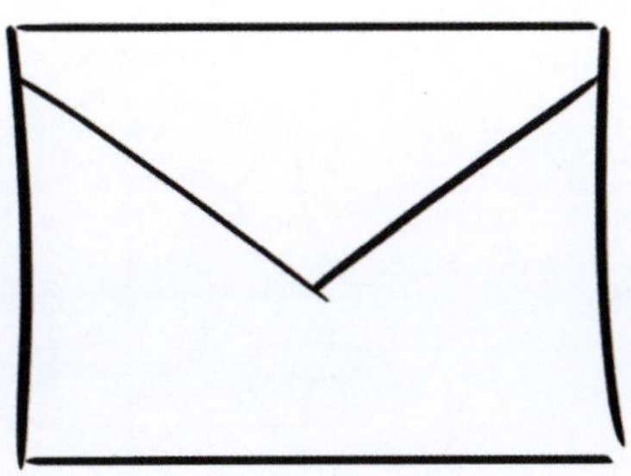

3

4

DAY 96

Cobweb

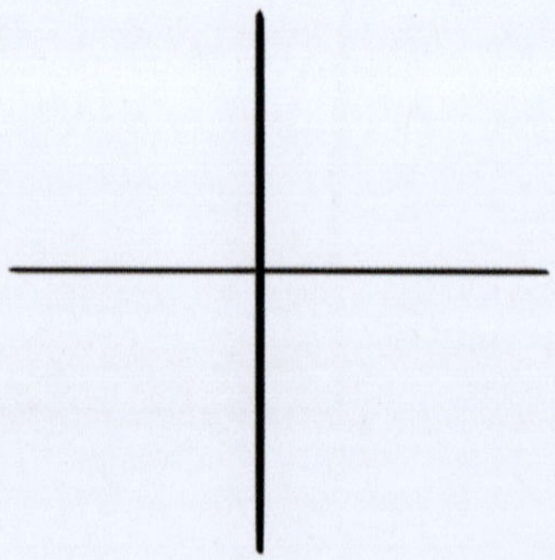

1

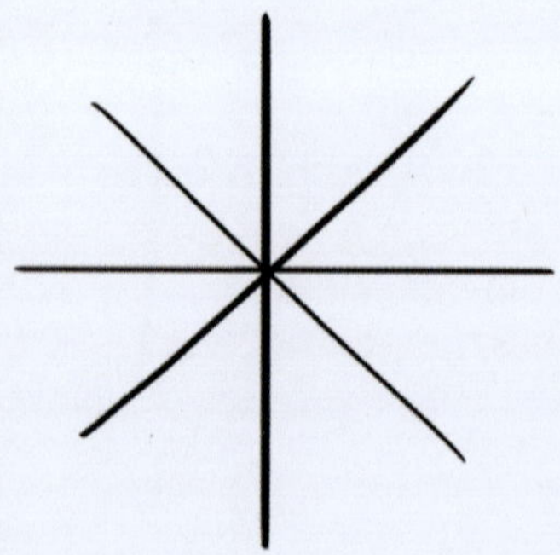

2

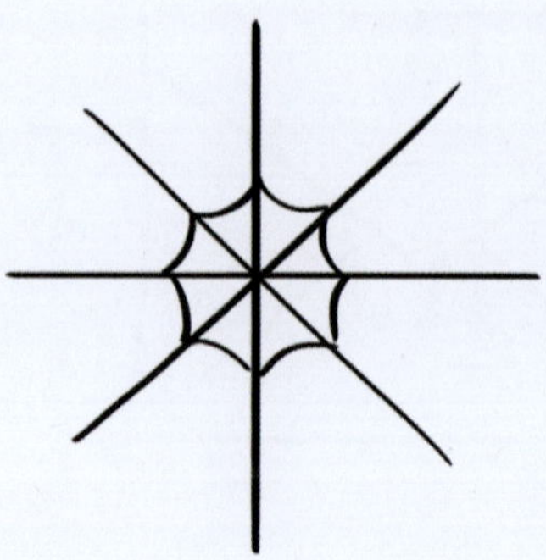

3

4

5

DAY 97

Card game

1

2

3

4

5

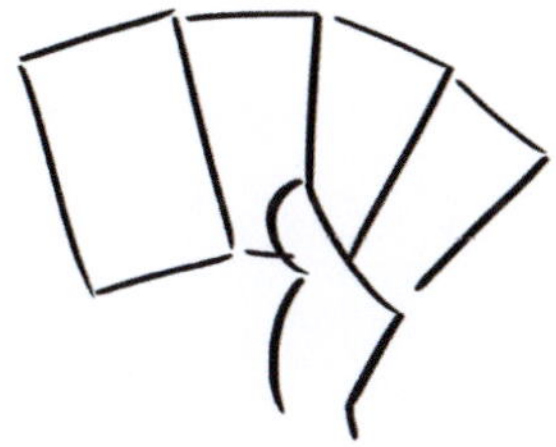

6

7

8

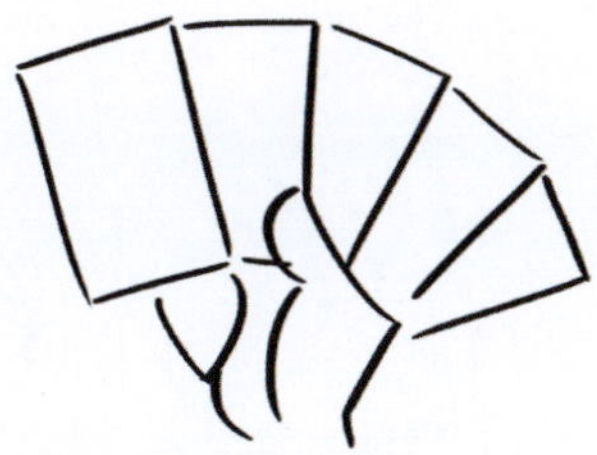

9

DAY 98

Monocycle

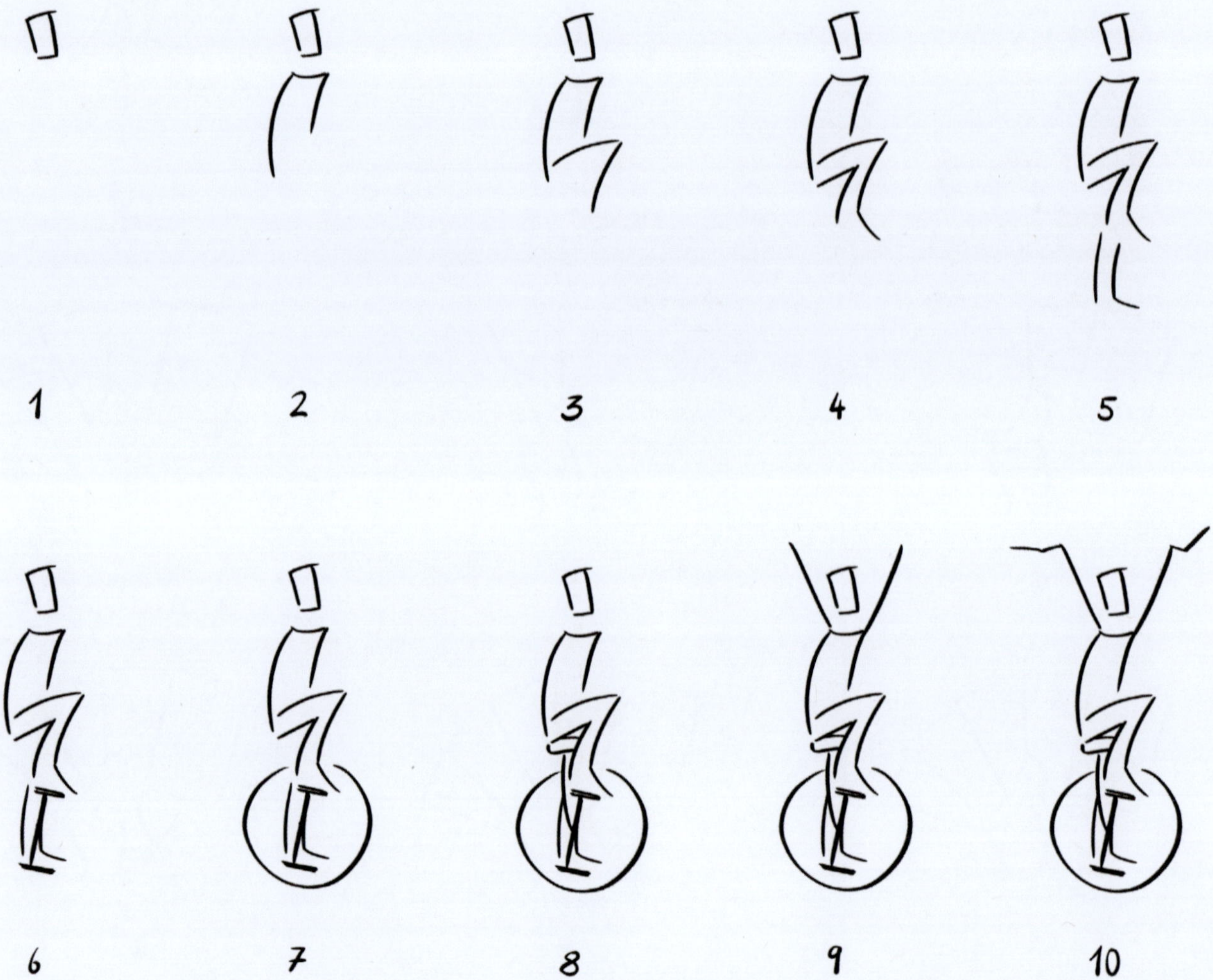

Needle and yarn

1

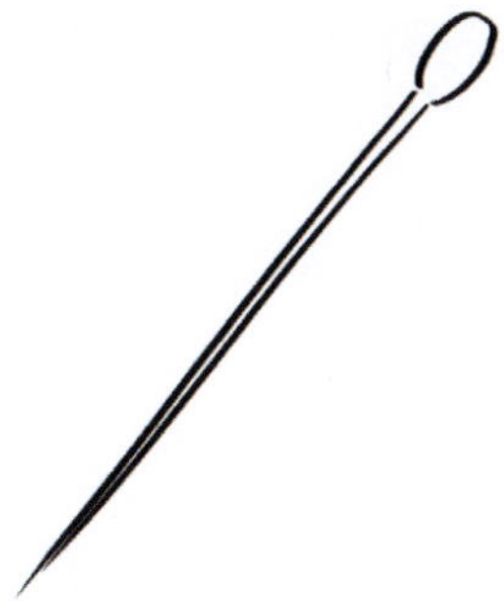

2

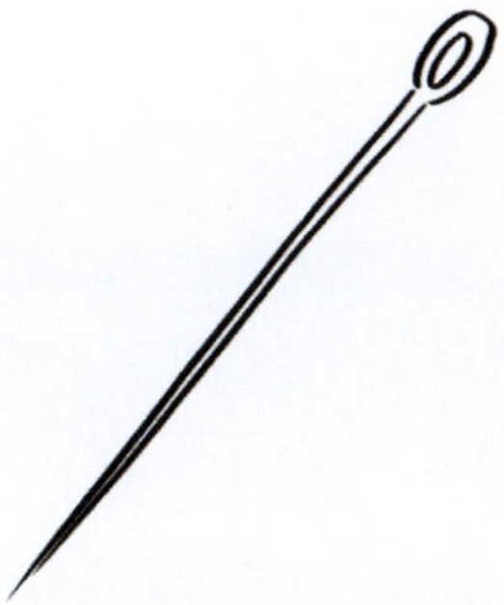

3

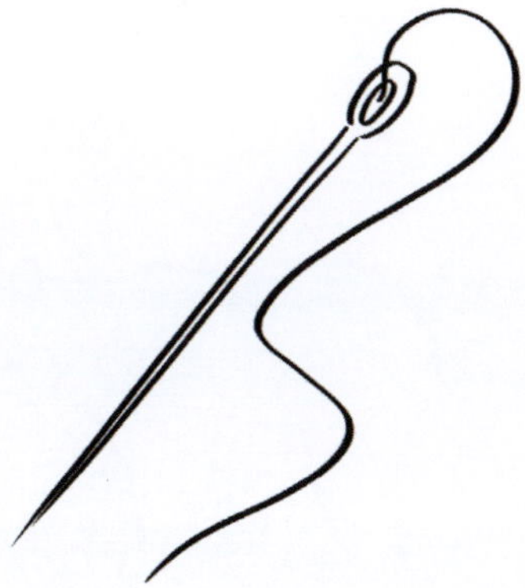

4

5

Bear

THANK YOU

For staying with us to the end! You've done it! Congratulations. I hope you had fun drawing and learning.
Write me at **holger@workvisual-institute.com** if you want to share your insights with me or have any questions. I'd love to hear from you and get to know you!

For more visual input follow my journey and what I do on **holgernilspohl.com** and subscribe to my newsletter. It's full of worthwhile content for you. :)

Some tips
for color and contrast

You create harmony if you use colors that are neighbors on the color wheel.

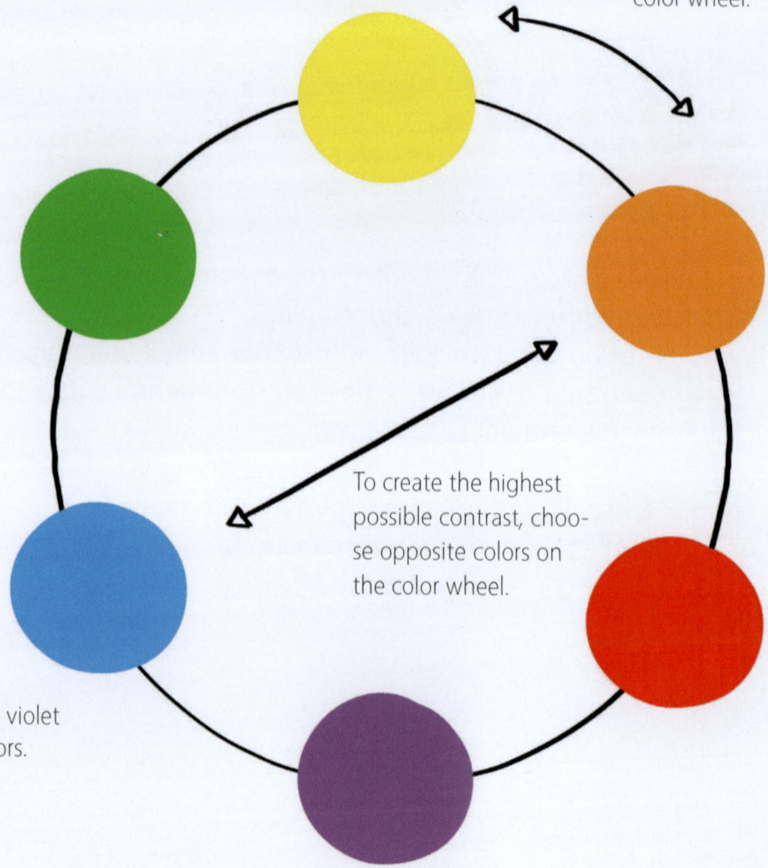

Yellow, orange and red are the warm colors.

To create the highest possible contrast, choose opposite colors on the color wheel.

Green, blue and violet are the cold colors.

The white space in a drawing can help for clarity. Don't fear lots of white space.

Black appears to pop out in front, whereas lighter grey stays in the background.

You can use that to your advantage in your drawings, if you draw for example arrows in a lighter color to keep a picturer clearer.

Printed in Great Britain
by Amazon

13802692R00063